Interfacing and
Scientific Data
Communications Experiments

n or bef
ve bel

Peter R. Rony   David G. Larsen

Jonathan A. Titus   Christopher A. Titus

Originally published as
Interfacing & Scientific Data Communications Experiments
by E&L Instruments, Inc., Derby, CT

Howard W. Sams & Co., Inc.

4300 WEST 62ND ST. INDIANAPOLIS, INDIANA 46268 USA

Copyright © 1979 by Peter R. Rony, David G. Larsen,
Jonathan A. Titus, and Christopher A. Titus

FIRST EDITION
FIRST PRINTING—1979

International Standard Book Number: 0-672-21546-2
Library of Congress Catalog Card Number: 78-057213

Printed in the United States of America.

Preface

Our purpose in writing this book has been to introduce you to the principles involved in the transfer of data using the *asynchronous-serial* data transfer technique. This technique is embodied in the Universal Asynchronous Receiver/Transmitter or UART integrated circuit, the device that we will discuss throughout this book. Since most computer systems communicate with other computers, remote instruments, teletypewriters, terminals, and other electronic devices through the use of this data transmission technique, it is an important topic for further investigation.

We have concentrated on the use of the UART chip, since it is widely available, relatively inexpensive, and easy to use and understand. In fact, even the newer computer-compatible communication integrated circuits still use the asynchronous-serial data transfer technique. Thus, a thorough understanding of the UART chip and its operation will greatly help you to understand the new communication chips that are available now, as well as those that will be available in the future.

One of the reasons that we are so interested in the use of asynchronous-serial data transmissions is that it is one of the most universal interfacing standards available today. There are very few general-purpose computers that do not have an asynchronous-serial input/output (I/O) port that can be readily adapted for communications with other computers and remote instruments. Asynchronous-serial data streams can be transmitted to orbiting satellites for retransmission to remote sites and vice versa, for very remote data acquisition that would be virtually impossible by any other means. Since more and more instruments and electronic data-acquisition systems are being made available with asynchronous-serial I/O ports, the task of interfacing these devices is reduced to the proper connection of from two to six wires. Still, software (computer programs) must be written to control these devices, but this is a subject for another book.

Much of our experience in the application of asynchronous-serial data transfers involved work done by Mr. David Larsen and Dr. Peter Rony and, separately, by Dr. Jon Titus. This book was originally published as *Bugbook® IIA* by E&L Instruments, Derby, CT, in early 1975. Since then it has been updated by the original authors, Mr. David G. Larsen and Dr. Peter R. Rony and recently it has been completely rewritten by Dr. Jon Titus, to include sections on clocks, oscillators, the USART and microcomputer applications. We hope that you will enjoy the book as it is now published.

Tychon, Incorporated is dedicated to educating the scientist, engineer, and electronics/computer hobbyist in the areas of digital electronics, microcomputer hardware and microcomputer software. We currently have monthly microcomputer columns appearing in *American Laboratory* (International Scientific Communications, Inc., 808 Kings Highway, Fairfield, CT 06430), *Computer Design, Radio-Electronics,* and *73 Magazine.* These columns also appear overseas in *Elettronica Oggi* (Italy), *Elektroniker* (Switzerland), *Electronic News* (Australia), and *Pulse* (Republic of South Africa). Some of our selected books have been translated into German, Italian, and Japanese, with translations into Spanish, Dutch, and other languages now underway.

If you are interested in learning basic digital electronics, a two-volume set of books in the *Blacksburg Continuing Education Series*™, entitled *Logic and Memory Experiments Using TTL Integrated Circuits,* will introduce you to the subject and give you the opportunity to perform student-tested experiments. Three other books in the series, *The 8080A Bugbook®* and the two volume set, *Introductory Experiments in Digital Electronics,* and *8080A Microcomputer Programming and Interfacing,* have been written about interfacing and programming 8080A-based computer systems. These self-teaching books describe the elementary hardware required for interfacing and they take the reader from simple input/output circuits through to complex priority interrupts. One of our latest books, *Microcomputer-Analog Converter Software and Hardware Interfacing,* is devoted to interfacing analog-to-digital and digital-to-analog converters to microcomputer systems. Complete interface circuits are provided along with complete software listings. Our most recent book, *8080/8085 Software Design,* provides over 190 specific program examples, as it delves into writing programs in assembly language for 8080 and 8085 processors.

There are many other titles in the *Blacksburg Continuing Education Series,* and we hope that you will have the opportunity to look them over. We continue to be interested in identifying potential authors who can contribute timely technical books to our series. If you have an interest in writing such a book, please contact us c/o Tychon in Blacksburg, Virginia.

Many of the concepts that are discussed in this book, and in our other books, as well, are presented in short course form by Tychon, Incorporated and by the Extension Division of the Virginia Polytechnic Institute and State University. If you are interested in these course offerings, please write to Dr. Chris Titus at Tychon, Inc., P. O. Box 242, Blacksburg, VA 24060, or Dr. Linda Leffel at the Donaldson Brown Center for Continuing Education, VPI&SU, Blacksburg, VA 24061.

"The Blacksburg Group"   PETER R. RONY
                               DAVID G. LARSEN
                               JONATHAN A. TITUS
                               CHRISTOPHER A. TITUS

Contents

Interfacing and Scientific Data Communications Experiments

INTRODUCTION TO SERIAL DATA COMMUNICATIONS

Most communications, whether from person-to-person, telephone exchange-to-telephone exchange, or computer to peripheral are serial in nature. Thus, words, signals, and data are all "transmitted" serially, one at a time and "received" serially. It is impossible to imagine a complete sentence being communicated in parallel, since this would mean that each word would have to be spoken at the same time. In fact, most communication is a serial transfer of "data," from a source to a destination.

Our purpose in this book is to describe the specialized use of serial data transfers between electronic instruments, peripherals, computers, terminals, and other electronic devices. Our focus may seem narrow, but a fundamental understanding of the serial transfer of data is important for many reasons, as you will discover throughout this book.

The electrical transfer of information is fairly old, having its beginning in the serial transmission of Morse code over a pair of wires between telegraph or railway offices. Actually, serial data transmissions have a long history, going back to the use of runners, smoke signals, and heliographs.

Let us imagine for a moment the transmission of a message in Morse code from one telegraph station to another. We will assume that a direct electrical path exists between the two stations. How does the transmission actually start? The "transmitter" probably started not by sending the message itself, but rather by sending some sort of attention-getting code or sequences of dots and dashes. This would allow the receiver to get into position to start receiving the message.

After the initial attention-getting message was sent, perhaps some preamble was also sent, such as "Message follows . . ." This would prepare the receiver for the actual start of the message. The message was sent next and at the end, perhaps some additional information was added by the transmitter to indicate that the message had ended.

Actually, almost all serial exchanges take place in this way. In the telegraph example, the data that were transmitted were *asynchronous,* since there was no synchronization between the transmitter and receiver. The transmitter assumed that the receiver could follow or "copy" his Morse code transmissions. This will also be the case in all of the experiments and examples that we present in this book. All of the serial data transfers will be asynchronous. The alternative to asynchronous data transfers is *synchronous* data transfers. In this case, the transmitter and receiver are *synchronized,* or placed in step by some means. We will not discuss synchronous data transfers in this book. This type of data transfer occurs between large computers and specialized terminals, or between two large computers that are some distance apart.

In this book, we will show you how *asynchronous-serial* data communications techniques are used to transfer data between computers, instruments, teletypewriters, terminals, etc. We have assumed that you have a fundamental understanding of basic digital electronics and the SN7400-series transistor-transistor logic (TTL) integrated circuits. Even without this hands-on experience, this book can be valuable if you wish to learn more about how asynchronous-serial data transfers take place.

OBJECTIVES

At the end of this book, you will:

- Know why an asynchronous-serial data transfer can take place between two electronic devices without the use of a common, or synchronizing, clock.

- Be able to describe the operation of the UART integrated circuit for both the transmission and reception of asynchronous-serial information.

- Be able to describe the format of the serial bit stream transmitted by the UART.

- Be able to program a UART chip for various formats of data bits, stop bits, and parity.

- Be able to wire and use a UART circuit.

- Be able to describe the various kinds of clock circuits that may be used with UART and USART integrated circuits.

- Be able to describe the operation and programming of a USART-type integrated circuit.

- Be able to sketch and describe computer interfaces for both UART and USART devices.

- Be able to describe the computer programs that are used to control UARTs and USARTs.

- Be able to describe the operation of the parity bit in the asynchronous-serial transfer of data.

- Be able to discuss the use of 20-mA current loop and RS-232C (EIA) voltage signals for the transfer of digital information.

- Be able to wire and use several kinds of current loops.

- Be able to define simplex, half-duplex, and full-duplex data communications.

USING ASYNCHRONOUS-SERIAL DATA TRANSFERS

Interfacing can be defined as the joining of members of a group (such as people, instruments, etc.) in such a way that they are able to function in a compatible and coordinated way. A knowledge of interfacing fundamentals has only recently become mandatory for students, engineers, scientists, and even hobbyists who are interested in using terminals, computers, and other digital instruments and devices. In the 1950s, when digital instruments were virtually unknown, the interfacing task was a simple one: analog signals were connected between instruments by standard cables. A sound knowledge of impedance-matching, noise reduction, group loops, and amplification generally was required to interface instruments properly.

Today, the problem of interfacing two electronic devices has been magnified as a direct consequence of the many new options available to the scientist, engineer, student, and computer user. In addition to what might be called the analog-to-analog interface, which we have mentioned above, we now have the option of interfacing analog instruments to digital ones, digital instruments to analog ones, and most importantly, digital instruments to other digital instruments or digital computers. In this last category, to compound the problem, there exist (a) a variety of digital codes with which this interfacing may be accomplished, i.e., binary coded decimal, binary, ASCII, etc., (b) a variety of modes of data transmission, i.e., parallel, asynchronous serial and synchronous serial, and (c) the necessity for several digital control signals that are required to synchronize the two digital devices so that they function in a "coordinated and compatible" way.

The simplest type of interface between two electronic devices is a direct wire between the two, as shown in Fig. 1. Only two or three

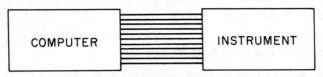

Fig. 1. Traditional computer-instrument interface.

wires may be required to transfer analog signals, while digital instruments may require as many as 50 or even 100 wires, depending on the number of control and data paths that are required to synchronize the two instruments for the meaningful transfers of data. Industrywide interfacing standards are still not available to permit the interfacing of one instrument to another through the use of a standardized multipin connector. The recently adopted IEEE-488 General Purpose Interface Bus (GPIB) standard is a step in the right direction, but this standard has not been widely accepted and it requires the transfer of a great deal of control information to make the interfaced instruments respond properly. In any case, it can be difficult to interface two instruments from two different manufacturers.

Multiwire, parallel digital data transmission, while suited for use in a situation in which instruments and computers are located close together, is not nearly as convenient an interfacing technique when the instruments are located at some distance from the central computer, or from each other. The cost of several hundred feet or several thousand feet of multiconductor cable becomes prohibitive. In such cases, the scheme shown in Fig. 2, in which a code converter, a receiver/transmitter and a transmission line are inserted between the instrument and the computer, can readily accomplish the interfacing at a modest cost.

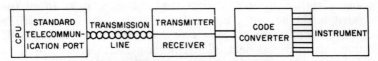

**Fig. 2. Use of two-wire transmission line
to interface instruments to computers.**

The transmission line shown in Fig. 2 is frequently one or two pairs of wires, perhaps twisted and shielded to reduce noise pickup. The mode of digital data transmission is called asynchronous serial, and its use is widespread in the telecommunications industry. We can best understand the popularity of the asynchronous-serial data transfer technique by inquiring as to what might be the least expensive way to transmit digital data from one place to another. We would probably conclude that a pair of wires would accomplish the task at minimum cost, provided that the digital data are sent sequentially, i.e., in a serial, rather than in a parallel format. We could probably assume that the cost of a "converter" that would convert the parallel data into a serial format, and the cost of a receiver/transmitter would be offset by the cost of the multiconductor cable that would otherwise be required to make all of the parallel connections. It is important to note that the telephone system in the United States is based on such pairs of wires and that it provides the potential for data transfers across thousands of miles.

When using the asynchronous-serial data transfer technique, digital data are sent from a transmitter to a receiver over a pair of wires. The data are represented by a "stream" of logic ones and logic zeros sent in a predetermined sequence. The data transfer rates are generally measured in the number of bits that are transferred each second. Data transfer rates from 50 to several thousand bits per second are quite common. The notation *baud* is frequently used to represent this rate, i.e., 2000 bits per second would be 2000 baud. The term *baud* may have several meanings, depending on the signalling techniques used. It actually represents the number of possible *condition changes* that can occur on a line in one second. In two-state (binary) signalling, the terms bits per second and baud may be used interchangeably, although we will use the bit-per-second notation in this book.

The serial data are transferred in some format that is compatible with the systems present at both the transmitter and receiver. Generally, data transfers take place using a standard coding format, some of which are described below:

Binary—A code of ones and zeros that represent numbers with weighted values of 2^x, where "x" is used to represent both positive and negative integers, i.e., $10101_2 = 21$.

Binary Coded Decimal—Each decimal digit is encoded apart from the others. The binary system is used to encode each digit. For example, $273 = 0010$ 0111 0011 (BCD).

ASCII (American Standard Code for Information Interchange)—A teletypewriter-based code in which binary numbers are used to represent specific typewriter-like symbols and characters, such as 1, $, A, and X.

EBCDIC (*Extended Binary Coded Decimal Interchange Code*)—A code that is similar to ASCII except that the various symbols are represented by different codes.

All of the above codes are binary, in the sense that they express information through the use of only the digits one and zero. Other codes may be used, as long as the transmitting and receiving devices have "agreed" on the specific code in use and its format. It is important to note, though, that the actual transmitter and receiver are "transparent" to the code being used. In the same way, an American-made telephone set may be used to converse with someone in German or Italian.

There are many applications for asynchronous-serial data transfers between instruments, computers, and peripheral devices. Here are some of the advantages of asynchronous-serial data transfers.

- The cost is low, generally only requiring one or two pairs of wires.

- Data rates in excess of 10,000 bits per second are possible.

- Generally, any instrument with a parallel binary output can be put "on-line" in a serial system.

- Little knowledge of digital electronics is required. This is particularly true of the Nationwide Electronics Systems, Inc., (Streamwood, IL 60103) "ASCII Bustle" which fits directly on their line of Slimline digital panel meters and permits the meters to be connected to a terminal using a single pair of wires.

- High-level programming languages such as BASIC, FORTRAN, and FOCAL are appropriate for use with asynchronous-serial interfaces for both data acquisition and control programming.

- Problems associated with the long-distance transmission of analog signals are overcome. Noise is reduced and shielded cables are generally not required.

- Interfacing the asynchronous-serial signals to a computer does not necessarily mean that the user must design and build the interface for a specific instrument. Standard telecommunication interfaces or "ports" are available from computer manufacturers so that the remote instrument may be readily interfaced with one or two pairs of wires.

- The system is easily expanded so that additional asynchronous-serial devices may be added and additional features, such as remote control, may be added at a later time.

- The asynchronous-serial transfer technique is compatible with modems and telephone couplers so that the technique may be used with almost any telephone line for remote data acquisition.

- Integrated circuits are available at low cost to simplify the standard asynchronous-serial interface designs, when one is required.

Most analytical instruments now have some sort of digital output that may be used to represent the value of the parameter being measured. In devices where these parallel data lines are not available, there may exist inexpensive, easy-to-use converters that can convert unknown analog signals to parallel, digitized values. For example, a three and one-half digit panel meter would have a total of thirteen output lines, as shown in Fig. 3. Each of the digits has been encoded in the binary coded decimal (BCD) format. It should be emphasized that these thirteen outputs are *parallel:* all of the digital information is available simultaneously. A range of outputs between 0000 and 1999 is possible. This is generally 0 to 1.999 volts or 0 to 1.999 millivolts, depending on the digital panel meter chosen.

A relatively inexpensive integrated circuit or "chip," the Universal Asynchronous Receiver/Transmitter or UART can take this parallel data and transmit it to a computer via the standard asynchronous communications port of the computer. The UART integrated circuit is available for under $10.00. There are many different types and configurations and we will introduce you to them as we describe each in the text.

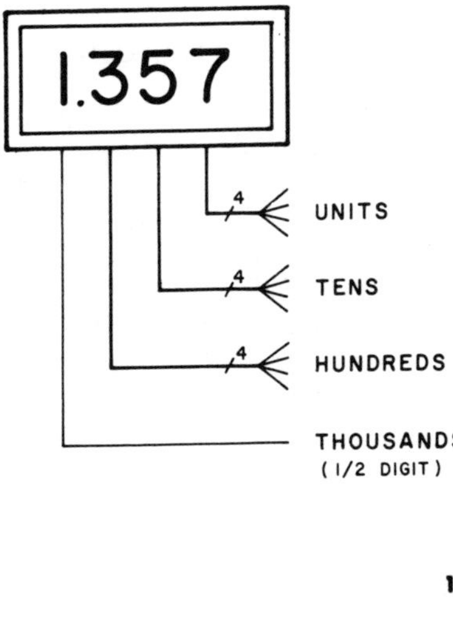

Fig. 3. Thirteen output lines from a "3½" digit panel meter with parallel binary coded decimal outputs.

1.357

UNITS
TENS
HUNDREDS
THOUSANDS
(1/2 DIGIT)

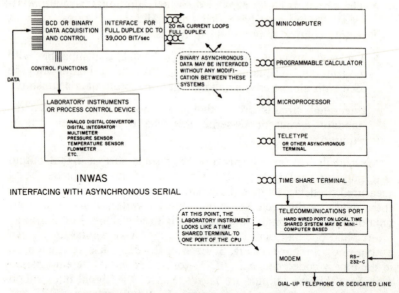

Fig. 4. Some of many possible interface schemes in which asynchronous-serial data transfers are used.

The information in Fig. 4 summarizes what we have been saying. By converting parallel data to serial data in a standard format, it is possible to interface an instrument or digital device to a Digital Equipment Corporation, Honeywell, NCR, IBM, Control Data, or other computer. Thus, it is possible to interface a device not only to a computer, but to a calculator, a microcomputer, a terminal, or a modem, as well.

ASYNCHRONOUS COMMUNICATIONS

Transmitting digital information over a pair of wires is not at all difficult. In fact, a simple parallel-to-serial shift register, such as the SN74165 can be used as a transmitter and a serial-to-parallel shift register, such as the SN74164 may be used as the receiver. All that is involved is the loading of the parallel data into the transmitter and shifting it out of the shift register, one bit at a time. The receiver would likewise shift the received data into the shift register, one bit at a time, until all of the bits had been received. Unfortunately, this is not an asynchronous transmission, since common clock signals and several control signals are required between the two shift register integrated circuits. It would work, however, but it would not be compatible with standard asynchronous-serial data transfer techniques. In a truly asynchronous data transfer, only the data transmission line connects the receiver and transmitter.

Obviously, there must be some "tricks" that are used to control the truly asynchronous-serial data transfers. We will explain these "tricks," or conventions, before we discuss their actual use.

Since there is not a common clock signal connected between the transmitter and receiver, and also no control signals between them, a START BIT always precedes any data transfer. This bit is *always* a logic zero. It is used to indicate to the receiver that a new series of data bits has been transmitted. Each data transmission ends with either one or two STOP BITS, which are *always* logic ones. The choice of one or two stop bits is somewhat arbitrary, as you will see. In some specialized applications, one and one-half stop bits may also be used.

Clearly, there must be some limit placed on the number of data bits in each transmission, otherwise some systems might try to transmit five data bits after the start bit, while others might wish to transmit several hundred. The series of data bits found between the start bit and the stop bit is limited to between five and eight data bits. A typical timing diagram for the transmission of an 8-bit data word is shown in Fig. 5. Note that the start bit is a logic zero and that two logic one stop bits have been transmitted. The least significant bit (LSB) has been transmitted just after the start bit. As an example, the 8-bit data word that is shown in Fig. 6 represents the binary word 10011101. An additional optional bit may be placed between the final data bit or most significant bit (MSB) and the stop bit.

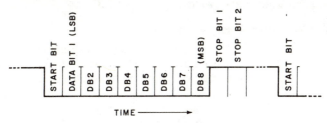

Fig. 5. Typical asynchronous-serial bit pattern (data bits may be logic 1 or 0).

This is the *parity bit,* which is used to check for errors in the data transmission. The parity bit indicates whether the number of logic ones in the data word is even or odd. The parity bit will be discussed in more detail in one of the experiments. In the notation used in this book, the *data bits* refer only to the five to eight bits of actual information contained in the bit stream. The start bit, parity bit, and stop bit(s) are not included in the representation, data bits.

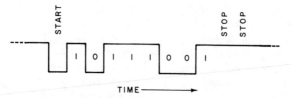

Fig. 6. Asynchronous-serial transmission of 8-bit data word, 10011101₂.

You can probably guess that there must be some standardization maintained between the transmitters and receivers. The transmission and reception rates must be closely aligned and the receiver must expect to receive the same number of data and control bits that the transmitter is actually going to be transmitting to it. Thus, you could *not* transfer asynchronous-serial data between devices that:

1. Have markedly different data transfer rates, i.e., a terminal with a data rate of 1200 bits per second and a computer with a data rate of 110 bits per second.
2. Were preset to have different numbers of data bits in the serial bit stream, i.e., a terminal that transmitted eight data bits and another terminal that expected to receive five bits of data.
3. Were preset to transmit and receive different kinds of parity information and serial bit streams with differing stop bit patterns. In this case, the data might be received, but the bits might not be what are expected.

Digital Transmitter/Receiver Circuits

Transmitter circuits that may be used to serialize parallel data and transmit it at the proper rate are not very difficult to visualize or to construct. An 11-bit parallel-to-serial shift register could be constructed with a hardwired start bit (logic zero) and two hardwired stop bits (logic ones), separated by positions for eight data bits. An appropriate clock signal, preset for the correct data transfer rate, could be used to shift the bits to the output of the shift register in a serial fashion. Such a scheme is illustrated in Fig. 7. Note that the Serial Input has been hardwired to a logic one. This is used to fill the shift register with logic ones while the data bits are being shifted out. Thus, even when the data word has been completely transmitted, along with the control bits, the transmitter will continue to transmit logic ones, the normal idle state for the asynchronous-serial communication line. Additional circuitry would have to be added to the circuit shown in Fig. 7 to synchronize the Load signal with the Clock input.

18

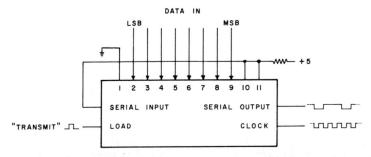

Fig. 7. Block diagram of 11-bit parallel-in, serial-out shift register used as simple asynchronous-serial transmitter.

The receiver circuitry is not quite as easy to visualize, since there is no common clock signal connected between it and the transmitter. Generally, the receiver sits in the idle mode. It does not start to perform any useful functions until it starts to receive the bits that have been transmitted to it. How does it know when it is to start to receive the bits, and how are they sampled?

You should now be able to see the purpose of the start bit. The receiver monitors its serial input line until it goes from the normal (idle) logic one state to the logic zero state, as it would at the beginning of the start bit. When such a transition has been sensed, the receiver waits for one-half of a bit period. The start bit is then tested again to be sure that it is still present. This testing is delayed by one-half of a bit period so that it will take place in about the center of the start bit. The following bits are then tested at intervals of one bit-time so that they are actually tested in the middle of their duration. This sampling technique allows for some "jitter" in the incoming signal, and also for small differences in the clock signals at the receiver and the transmitter. This difference must be less than 3%. The bit-time or bit-period is the time required for one bit to be transmitted at the data rate being used. Thus, for a 110 bit-per-second data transmission rate, the bit-time would be about 9.09 milliseconds.

In the same way that the receiver monitors for the presence of the start bit, also checks for the stop bit or bits to be sure that they occur where they should. You should note that the quiescent state or idle state of the input of the receiver is the logic one state.

Constructing a transmitter/receiver from standard logic integrated circuits or "chips" is not a trivial task. Prior to 1970, though, this is exactly what was done when these functions were required. In 1970, The Universal Asynchronous Receiver/Transmitter or UART was made available in integrated circuit form in a 40-pin dual in-line package so that asynchronous-serial data transfer became a readily usable communication technique.

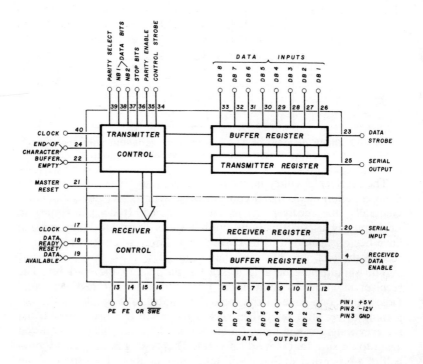

Fig. 8. Functional block diagram of UART (copyright, Ham Radio Magazine, 1976).

Universal Asynchronous Receiver/Transmitter (UART)

The Universal Asynchronous Receiver/Transmitter or UART has been developed so that almost all of the receiver/transmitter circuitry is incorporated within a standard 40-pin integrated-circuit package. A functional block diagram of the UART is shown in Fig. 8. There are many functions within the chip that are readily preset or "programmed" by the user so that many different formats of asynchronous-serial data can be accommodated.

In the following paragraphs, we will describe the operation of the UART so that you will understand its operation. This understanding is important, since it will allow you to quickly grasp the principles that are used in the experiments at the end of the book. The functions of the generalized UART chip that we will describe are applicable to all of the UART-type chips available. Our discussion will center on TMS6012 manufactured by Texas Instruments, the

TR1602 by Western Digital Corporation, and the AY-3-1015 produced by General Instrument Corporation. In many cases, the nomenclature used by the various UART manufacturers varies from device to device. Do not let this concern you. The pin numbers and the functional descriptions will all be the same for compatible devices. For this reason, we have noted the pin numbers, along with the applicable signal names, where needed. In all of our descriptions, the logic one state is assumed to be from 2.8 volts to 5 volts and the logic zero state is assumed to be ground to 0.8 volt. These are standard TTL-compatible levels.

UART Control

The UART control signals are those that are common to both the transmitter and receiver sections. These include the MASTER RESET, pin 21, and six other control signals that will be described separately. The six control signals control the format of the data being transmitted *and* received. The formats for the receiver and the transmitter sections of each chip are the same, since the same six lines are used to program them both. Keep in mind the fact that if different data formats are required, two or more UART chips will be needed.

We will now describe the control signals and the function of each:

MASTER RESET (pin 21): A logic one on this input will reset the UART chip. This input must be at the logic zero state for normal operation. The UART should be reset whenever power is applied to it.

No PARITY (pin 35): A logic one on this input will eliminate the presence of the parity bit in the transmitted stream of bits. Likewise, the receiver will not expect to receive a parity bit in the incoming stream of bits. If this bit is a logic zero, the parity bit, even or odd, will be placed in the serial stream of bits between the last data bit (MSB) and the stop bit(s). Likewise, the receiver will expect to receive a parity bit if pin 35 is a logic zero.

PARITY SELECT (pin 39): A logic one on this input selects the even parity mode and a logic zero selects the odd parity mode. The mode selection is not used by the internal logic of the UART if the No Parity input (pin 35) is in the logic one state.

NUMBER OF STOP BITS (pin 36): A logic zero at this input will select one stop bit, while a logic one will select two stop bits.

NUMBER OF DATA BITS (pins 37 and 38): These pins allow the selection of five, six, seven or eight data bits in the serial stream of bits, between the start bit and the stop bit(s). If five data bits are selected, then there will be five data bits in the transmitted information and the receiver section of the UART will expect to receive five data bits. These two inputs are programmed as follows:

NB-2 (pin 37)	NB-1 (pin 38)	Data Bits
0	0	5*
0	1	6
1	0	7
1	1	8

* In the TR1602 UART device, the selection of five data bits and two stop bits will actually cause one and one-half stop bits to be generated.

The TR1602 UART device may be programmed for five data bits and one and one-half stop bits, i.e., a logic one at the end of the transmission for a minimum of one and one-half bit times. This is frequently used when the five-level or five-bit Baudot code is being used, as is the case in some types of radioteletype (RTTY) communications.

CONTROL STROBE (pin 34): A logic one on this input to the UART will enter the five control bits into the control circuitry of the UART. This input may be pulsed with a logic one, or it may be hardwired to a logic one, as is usually the case. The Control Strobe may also be pulsed, under the control of the instrument or computer that is using it, so that different control bit settings may be programmed into the UART.

The UART Transmitter

CLOCK (pin 40): The UART transmitter section accepts a parallel set of up to eight data bits, formats them with control bits, and then sends them in a serial bit stream. To do this, it first requires a clock signal. In most UART applications, the clock signal must be 16 times the serial data rate. Thus, for a 1200 bit-per-second transmission rate, a 19,200-Hz clock signal would be required. The clock signal of the transmitter is applied to pin 40 as a TTL-compatible square wave.

DATA STROBE (pin 23): The UART transmitter section also uses three control signals to control the actual transmission of the serial information. The Data Strobe (pin 23) is a signal that loads the 8-bit data word into the Transmitter Buffer Register. A logic zero on the Data Strobe input causes this action to take place. If the transmitter is still transmitting data, the current transmission is completed before the newly entered data is transferred from the Transmitter Buffer Register to the Transmitter Register, from which it is transmitted.

TRANSMITTER BUFFER EMPTY (pin 22): A Transmitter Buffer Empty signal (TBMT) or flag is provided as an output to indicate that the Transmitter Buffer Register is either empty (logic one) or that it still contains a data word that has yet to be transmitted (logic zero). When a data word has been transferred from the Transmitter

Buffer Register to the Transmitter Register for transmission, the Transmitter Buffer Empty flag output goes to a logic one, indicating that the next data word may be entered into the transmitter section of the UART.

END OF CHARACTER (pin 24): An additional flag output is provided to indicate whether or not a transmission is in progress. The End of Character flag (EOC) is a logic one when there is no transmission taking place and it is a logic zero when a character is being transmitted. The character is the 5- to 8-bit data word and the control bits, as well. Note that the transmitter section is comprised of two registers, so that it may be transmitting one character while another one is waiting. This is called *double buffering*.

SERIAL OUTPUT (pin 25): The serial output (SO) from the transmitter is available at pin 25. This serial output is a TTL-compatible representation of the bit stream.

The UART Receiver

CLOCK (pin 17): The receiver section of the UART is somewhat more complex than that of the transmitter section, since start bits, stop bits, parity bits, and data bits must be recognized and acted on. Much of this has been previously discussed. The receiver section also requires a clock signal that is 16 times the bit rate that will be received. The clock signal of the receiver is applied to pin 17. If the transmitter and the receiver will be used at the same data rates, pins 17 and 40 may be connected to a common clock signal.

RECEIVED DATA ENABLE (pin 4): Once a serial stream of bits has been received, it is transferred in parallel, from the Receiver Register to the Buffer Register in the receiver section of the UART. The eight data outputs from this section are three-state-type outputs. Three-state means that the outputs may be in either their normal logic one or logic zero state, or they may be in a high impedance state, the third state. This high impedance state disconnects the receiver outputs of the UART from the device that they are connected to so that the electrical connection is essentially "broken." This is useful, as you will see later. The Received Data Enable (RDE) input at pin 4 must be a logic zero to make the received digital data available on the eight outputs from the Buffer Register of the receiver. If the Received Data Enable input is a logic one, these eight data outputs will be placed in the high impedance state, disconnecting them from the system.

DATA READY RESET (pin 18) and RECEIVED DATA AVAILABLE (pin 19): The availability of the parallel data from a completely received transmission is indicated by the state of the Received Data Available flag (RDA), pin 19. A logic one at this output indicates that a complete set of data bits has been received and transferred to the receiver Buffer Register. A logic zero indicates that a set of data bits has not been received yet. A Data Ready Reset flag (DRR), pin 18, is available as an input so that the Received Data Available flag may be reset after the flag has been sensed and the data have been used by the receiving system. This action readies the Received Data Available flag so that it may be used to sense the availability of the next set of data bits that will be sent serially to the receiver section of the UART. A logic zero applied to the Data Ready Reset input will reset the Received Data Available flag. The Data Ready Reset input may sometimes be called the Reset Data Available flag.

The receiver section of the UART also has three outputs that are used to indicate possible error conditions. These outputs or flags are:

PARITY ERROR (pin 13): This output goes to a logic one state if the parity of the received data word does not agree with the parity that has been selected for the UART at pin 39, Parity Select. The Parity Error output is meaningless if no parity has been selected, as would be the case if the No Parity control pin, pin 35, were a logic one.

FRAMING ERROR (pin 14): A logic one at this output is used to indicate that the receiver did not detect a stop bit, or two stop bits, in the received stream of bits.

OVERRUN (pin 15): A logic one at this output indicates that the Received Data Available flag was not reset after the previous character had been received. Thus, the character just received has written over the one received prior to it. This assumes, of course, that the receiving circuitry, external to the UART, resets the Received Data Available flag after each new data word is sensed and "used." This is generally the case.

STATUS WORD ENABLE (pin 16): The Parity Error, Overrun Error and Framing Error flags, as well as the Transmitter Buffer Empty and Received Data Available flags, all have three-state outputs. These outputs are all controlled simultaneously by the Status Word Enable input, pin 16. When this input is at a logic zero, the outputs of all five flags are active (logic one or logic zero), but if the Status Word Enable input is at a logic one, the five flag outputs assume the high impedance or "disconnected" state. If you will not be using the three-state capability that is available, we suggest that you ground pins 4 and 16 of the UART. This will permanently enable the status and data outputs of the UART.

A few additional notes about the UART integrated circuit are needed before you can explore the use of the device.

Power Requirements: First-generation UART devices such as the TMS6011, TR1602, and AY-3-1015 require two power supplies, +5 volts (V_{ss}, pin 1), −12 volts (V_{gg}, pin 2) and a ground connection (V_{dd}, pin 3). Second generation devices require only the

+5-volt and ground connections. An example of such a device is the Western Digital TR1863A or General Instruments AY-3-1014A.

Data Format: The Asynchronous-serial data format requires that the least significant bit directly follow the start bit in the serial bit stream. The bit/pin designations are shown in Fig. 8, with RD-1 and DB-1 representing the least significant bit in the receiver and transmitter data, respectively. When fewer than eight data bits are selected, the least significant bits are used by the transmitter and receiver sections. Thus, if a 5-bit data word is to be transmitted, the five data bits are applied to the five least significant bits of the transmitter input pins. The received data are found on the five least significant data bits of the receiver buffer register and the unused data outputs of the receiver assume the logic one state. The transmitter, of course, does not transmit the unused bits.

Clock: The clock signal to both the transmitter and receiver sections of the UART is generally a square wave generated by a crystal oscillator, or by a stable R/C-based clock. The maximum *clock rate* will vary from one type of UART chip to another. The Western Digital TR1863A chip has a maximum clock rate of 1.0 MHz for a maximum data rate of 62,500 bits per second. The General Instruments AY-3-1014A UART has a maximum clock rate of 480 kHz, for a maximum data rate of 30 kilobits per second. Remember that in almost all cases, the clock rate of the UART will be 16 times the data rate. You will find that the transmission line bandwidth, or data capacity, is generally the limiting factor, and not the speed of the UART.

Inputs/Outputs: The inputs and outputs of the UART are all compatible with the transistor-transistor logic (TTL) family, so they are readily used with standard SN7400-, SN74L00-, and SN74LS00-type devices. The UART outputs can generally drive one standard SN7400-series input, giving it a fan-out of one. Each of the UART inputs should be considered as having a fan-in of one. For additional information about the UART, we suggest that you examine specific data sheets from the various manufacturers. A sample UART data sheet has been provided in the appendix.

To summarize all of the UART signal nomenclature and pin numbering, we have included this information in Table 1.

The Complimentary Metal-Oxide Semiconductor UART Device

In some applications, the high power dissipation of the standard UART devices (300 milliwatts) may be excessive, particularly where it is desired to use the UART in a remote battery-powered application. A newer UART integrated circuit has been fabricated through the use of the complimentary metal-oxide semiconductor (CMOS) process. The CMOS-fabricated UART allows low power operation

Table 1. Description of UART Signals and Pin Identifications

POWER SUPPLY		
Pin Number	Name	Function
1	V$_{cc}$	Power supply input, +5 volts
2	V$_{gg}$	Power supply input, −12 volts
3	V$_{dd}$	Ground

TRANSMITTER		
Pin Number	Name	Function
26	DB-1	Data Bit 1, Least significant transmitter input bit
27	DB-2	Data Bit 2
28	DB-3	Data Bit 3
29	DB-4	Data Bit 4
30	DB-5	Data Bit 5
31	DB-6	Data Bit 6
32	DB-7	Data Bit 7

Pin Number	Name	Function
33	DB-8	Data Bit 8, Most significant transmitter input bit
40	CLOCK	Clock input at 16 times the data rate
25	SO	Serial output from the transmitter
22	TBMT	Transmitter Buffer Empty flag Logic 1 = Ready for another character Logic 0 = Buffer full
23	DS	Data Strobe. A logic zero initiates the loading of the transmitter and the transmission of data
24	EOC	End of Character flag Logic 1 = No transmission in progress Logic 0 = Transmission in progress

RECEIVER		
Pin Number	Name	Function
12	RD-1	Data Bit 1, least significant receiver output bit
11	RD-2	Data Bit 2
10	RD-3	Data Bit 3
9	RD-4	Data Bit 4
8	RD-5	Data Bit 5
7	RD-6	Data Bit 6
6	RD-7	Data Bit 7
5	RD-8	Data Bit 8, most significant receiver output bit
17	CLOCK	Clock input at 16 times the data rate
20	SI	Serial input to the receiver
4	RDE	Received Data Enable Logic 1 = High impedance outputs Logic 0 = Data on eight outputs
18	DRR	Data Ready Reset (Reset Data Available) Logic 1 = Normal Mode Logic 0 = Reset Received Data Available flag
19	RDA	Received Data Available Logic 1 = Character received and available Logic 0 = No character received

Table 1 Cont. Description of UART Signals and Pin Identifications

13	PE	Parity Error
		Logic 1 = Parity error detected
		Logic 0 = No parity error
14	FE	Framing Error
		Logic 1 = Framing error, no stop bits detected
		Logic 0 = No framing error
15	OR	Overrun Error
		Logic 1 = RDA flag not reset prior to receipt of a new set of data bits
		Logic 0 = No error

CONTROL		
Pin Number	**Name**	**Function**
21	MR	Master Reset. A logic one clears the UART.
34	CS	Control Strobe. A logic one loads the control bits into the UART.
35	NP	No Parity
		Logic 1 = No parity appended to the data
		Logic 0 = Parity bit appended to the data
39	PE	Parity or Parity Even
		Logic 1 = Even parity appended
		Logic 0 = Odd parity appended
36	SB	Stop bits
		Logic 1 = Two stop bits
		Logic 0 = One stop bit
37-38	NB-2	Number of data bits
	NB-1	
16	SWE	Status Word Enable. Controls the PE, FE, OR, RDA and TBMT flag outputs.
		Logic 1 = High impedance outputs
		Logic 0 = Status outputs enabled

Pin 37	Pin 38	Data Bits
0	0	5
0	1	6
1	0	7
1	1	8

(less than 1 milliwatt) and the UART has some features that are not found on other UART chips.

The Intersil IM6402 and IM6403 devices will be described briefly to highlight the differences between them and the standard UART chips. The internal receiver/transmitter functions are the same as those described previously. Serial data are transmitted and received in exactly the same manner. The main difference between these two types of UART devices is that the CMOS-type devices require only the +5-volt power supply. The −12-volt power supply is not required *and it must not be connected to these UART devices.* The outputs from the CMOS UARTs are able to power a standard 7400-series TTL load, but to do this, the power supply to the CMOS

UART must be +5 volts. We might add, too, that the Western Digital TR1863A and TR1863B UART devices also require just the +5-volt power supply, but they dissipate 18 milliwatts.

There are some substantial differences between the CMOS UARTs and other types of UART chips. These non-CMOS UARTs are generally fabricated by using the p-channel metal-oxide semiconductor technology and are often called PMOS devices. This is irrelevant to our discussion, although you may see the term PMOS in some UART data sheets.

The nomenclature from the UART devices that have been previously discussed has been preserved. It is important for you to note that the PMOS and CMOS UARTs are not pin-for-pin compatible. A CMOS UART that is placed in a socket intended for a PMOS UART will be destroyed on the application of power. A complete CMOS UART data sheet has been provided in the appendix. You may wish to refer to it as we discuss some of the CMOS UART functions.

There are some subtle differences between the two Intersil CMOS UARTs, the IM6402 and IM6403, that require some additional explanation. The main difference between these UARTs and the PMOS UARTs is that the CMOS devices do not require the −12-volt power supply. This is actually the only difference between the IM6402 UART and PMOS UARTs.

The IM6403 CMOS UART has some additional features that you may find interesting. These are the availability of an on-chip oscillator, a clock divider control and non-three-state outputs for two of the status flags. The on-chip oscillator is operated by placing an external crystal between pins 17 and 40, the pins that are generally used for the transmitter and receiver clock inputs. An internal oscillator generates the basic frequency of the crystal. This frequency may be divided by either 16 or 2048 to generate the clock signal that will be used to control both the receiver and the transmitter. This is the clock frequency and not the data rate or data frequency. Thus, an inexpensive color TV crystal that oscillates at 3.5795 MHz may be used with the divide-by-2048 to generate a clock signal that will cause the UART to transmit and receive data at a rate of 109.2 bits per second, within 3% of the 110-bit-per-second rate generally associated with teletypewriters. The IM6403 UART pin 2 input controls the divider stages. If this pin is at the logic one state, the divide-by-16 is placed in the frequency path and, if this pin is at the logic zero state, the divide-by-2048 is placed in the frequency path. In this way, there is a choice between two data rates, at your option.

The Received Data Available flag of the IM6403 UART receiver and the Transmitter Buffer Empty flag of the transmitter are not provided with three-state outputs, so if the three-state capability is required, external three-state buffers must be added to the circuit. A data sheet that covers both the IM6402 and IM6403 CMOS UART devices has been included in the appendix. You may wish to examine it in more detail. The CMOS UARTs may be substituted for the standard PMOS devices used in the experiments at the end of this book. We caution you not to connect the CMOS UARTs to the −12-volt power supply and, due to the differences between the IM6402 and IM6403 CMOS UARTs, we suggest that only the IM6402 be used as a substitute. The IM6403 would require additional changes that make it impractical for use in a general experimental situation. You may wish to breadboard the IM6403, but we suggest that you do so with caution, if you attempt to follow the experiments in this book.

The CMOS UARTs are currently being manufactured by:

Harris Semiconductor   HD-6402, HD-6403, HD-6402A,
Box 883   and HD-6403A
Melbourne, FL 32901

Intersil, Inc.   IM6402, IM6403, IM6402A,
10900 N. Tantau Avenue   and IM6403A
Cupertino, CA 95014

Clocks and Oscillators

As you are probably aware, the UART device requires a stable source of periodic clock pulses to enable it to operate properly. The source of the clock signal may be already present in the system that you are designing or working with, or perhaps it can be derived from another available clock signal through the use of counters and flip-flops to divide the clock signal so that it would have the desired frequency. In some cases, you will have to add a clock to your system. In any case, the main points to remember are:

- The clock must provide regular, periodic square waves at a frequency that is 16 times the required data rate, in bits per second.
- The stability and frequency of the clock must be such that the actual frequency is within 3% of the desired frequency to ensure accurate data transmission and reception.

As mentioned previously, dividers such as the SN7490 and SN74390 decade or SN7493 and SN74393 binary counters can also be used to derive the clock signal from one that is already present in the system in which the UART is to be used. In some cases, the basic clock frequency in a system may be slightly altered by changing the crystal that controls the main clock, so that the standard data transfer rates are obtained. There are other dividers that may be used for this function, the Mostek MK5009 and Exar XR2240 being typical examples.

If there is no clock available with the proper frequency, there are two types of clocks that may be designed into the system to provide the needed clock pulses for the UART chips. Either a crystal-based clock may be used or an R/C clock may be used. We have provided an example of each in the subsections that follow.

Crystal Clock

The Motorola MC4024 oscillator chip may be used with a crystal to provide a basic frequency that can be used by itself, or divided by a series of counters, to provide the clock signal that is needed by the UART chip. In the example shown in Fig. 9, a frequency of 1760 Hz is produced so that the UART can transmit and receive data at the rate of 110 bits per second. Note that the last stage of the divider chain is a divide-by-two stage so that the output of the clock is a symmetric square wave. The MC4042 oscillator integrated circuit

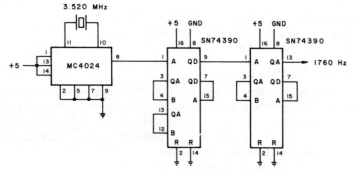

Fig. 9. Crystal-controlled clock using Motorola MC4024 oscillator and two SN74390 dual-decade counters.

has two independent oscillator sections so that a single chip may be used to generate two clock signals. Only one of the oscillator sections has been used, as shown in Fig. 9.

In the second example of a crystal clock, a Motorola MC14411 integrated circuit "Bit Rate Generator" is used. This chip includes the oscillator and the appropriate dividers in a single package. One of the features of this device is its ability to generate 16 different frequencies at the same time. While the frequencies are all different, they are all derived from the basic frequency of the crystal used with the MC14411. The bit rate generator chip also allows for the selection of clock rates that are 1, 8, 16, or 64 times the desired bit

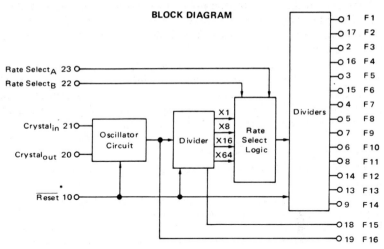

*Outputs go to "1" level upon reset.

PIN ASSIGNMENT

V_{DD} = Pin 24
V_{SS} = Pin 12

Fig. 10. Block diagram and pin configuration for Motorola MC14411 Bit Rate Generator Chip (copyright, Motorola Semiconductor).

rate. The pin configuration of the MC14411 bit rate generator chip is shown in Fig. 10, along with a block diagram of the circuit used.

A typical circuit in which the MC14411 is used is shown in Fig. 11. In this example, a frequency for a UART operating at 2400 bits per second is generated. Since the MC14411 can power only one low-power TTL input, such as the one found in the SN74L00-series

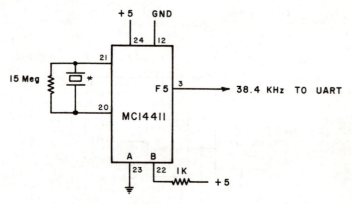

**Fig. 11. Typical application of MC14411 Bit Rate
Generator for 2400 bit per second UART.**

integrated circuits, we suggest that you "buffer" the clock signal with
some SN74L04 inverters. This has not been shown in Fig. 11, for
clarity.

R/C Clocks

Stable resistor/capacitor, or R/C, clocks can be used quite successfully with UART devices for the generation of the required
clock frequencies. We have used the popular NE555 Timer integrated circuit in many applications. If good quality components,
with low temperature coefficients, are chosen, the NE555 Timer chip
will provide reproducible square waves that may be used by the
UART chip. We recommend the use of resistors with a 1% tolerance and polypropylene or Teflon capacitors for high stability. A
typical example of this type of clock circuit is shown in Fig. 12. The
circuit shown is preset to provide a frequency of 1760 Hz. The 5-

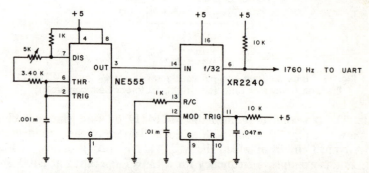

**Fig. 12. Typical R/C-type clock circuit (XR2240 provides
appropriate binary-divider stages).**

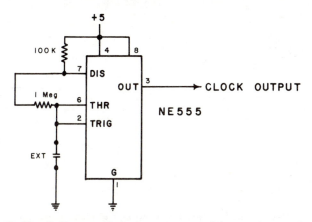

Fig. 13. Circuit diagram of clock recommended for use in experiments (EXT capacitor must be added for frequency needed).

kilohm trimmer resistor provides a means for adjusting the actual frequency of the clock. As shown in Fig. 12, an Exar 2240 divider has been used to divide the frequency to the final value required.

A similar clock circuit is shown in Fig. 13. We recommend this circuit if you are planning to perform the experiments in this book. It may be wired on a solderless breadboard, or the LR-5 Outboard module may be used instead. Various capacitors with values between 20 and 220 picofarads (pF) and between 0.01 and 0.5 microfarad (μF) will be used in the experiments. We suggest that you have an assortment available.

UART Applications

Now that you are familiar with the UART chip itself, we will describe a typical application so that you can see how the UART is used.

As you have probably guessed, the UART does not have to be used for data transfers, alone, in the sense that encoded ASCII or EDCDIC messages are transferred back and forth between terminals and computers. In this application, a remote UART is used to transmit alarm limit switch information and to receive control information. A local UART is used to receive the limit switch information and to transmit the control information to the remote UART. Such a configuration is shown in Fig. 14.

The alarm limit switches are connected to the eight UART transmitter data inputs, supplying TTL-compatible logic levels that indicate that each switch is either open or closed. This information is transmitted to the local UART, which displays the state of each switch by the use of light-emitting diodes (LEDs) that are connected

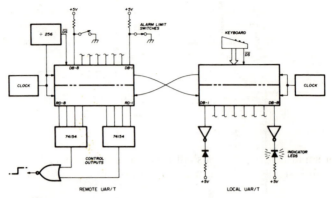

Fig. 14. UART used for remote sensing of eight inputs and for remote control (copyright, *Ham Radio Magazine,* 1976).

to the eight data outputs provided by the receiver section of the local UART chip. This is certainly a nonstandard use for a UART, but it allows us to monitor the state of eight switches by using only a single pair of wires. The transmitter strobe pulse (DS) is derived from the clock signal that drives the remote UART transmitter and receiver sections. If the divide-by-256 circuit is used with a UART that is transmitting data at a rate of 2400 bits per second, the switches are sampled 150 times each second.

The transmitter section of the local UART is connected to a keyboard. The keyboard may be encoded in any format, as long as the code for each key is known. The keyboard generates its own Data Strobe signal that loads the parallel data from the keyboard into the transmitter and initiates the serial transmission of the key code. We shall assume that an 8-bit key code is used in this scheme.

The eight parallel outputs from the remote UART receiver section are divided into groups of four lines each. These lines are connected to two SN74154 four-line-to-sixteen-line decoder integrated circuits. By gating one output from one decoder with one output from the other decoder, up to 256 individual outputs are available, one at a time. Each key code may be decoded at the remote UART to provide such a control signal to strobe a device, open a gate, turn on a valve, turn off a fan, etc. Only one control signal has been shown in Fig. 14, but others are possible, through the use of OR or NOR gates to gate together one output from each decoder. It is important to note that if this kind of a decoding scheme is used, only one of the possible 256 control signals is active at any time.

The control signals can also be generated in the same way in which the limit switches are sensed. Eight switches can be used at the local UART to control eight devices that are located at the remote UART. In this configuration, as with the limit switches, eight devices can be controlled simultaneously. Note that the clocks at both the local and remote UART must be the same, i.e., 38.4 kHz for a transmission of 2400 bits per second.

Microcomputer—UART Interfacing

While the UART integrated circuits can be used by themselves or with other kinds of circuitry, they are frequently used with computers to provide the essential interface between the computer and terminals and teletypewriters. Since there is so much interest in the use of small computers, we shall describe a typical UART interface. We shall also describe the use of one of the more advanced communication interface chips in another section. We have assumed that you are already somewhat familiar with microcomputer interfacing and software techniques. If you are not, we recommend, *The 8080A Bugbook®: Microcomputer Interfacing and Programming* (Howard W. Sams & Co., Inc., Indianapolis, IN 46206, 1977).

In this example, we have chosen to illustrate the use of the Western Digital TR1863A UART chip with an 8080A-based microcomputer. Other types of UARTs could have been used, as well. We have taken advantage of the three-state outputs on the UART receiver data outputs and on the various flag outputs. Thus, these outputs can be directly connected to the microcomputer data bus lines. This is illustrated in Fig. 15.

In this example, the UART is programmed so that the data stream contains eight data bits, no parity bit and two stop bits, in addition to the start bit. This selection is hardwired at the control pins of the UART, pins 34 through 39. Note that the transmitter data input lines, the receiver data output lines and the flag output lines are all connected to the 8080A computer data bus, in parallel. This is quite proper, since the inputs and outputs are not selected at the same time.

The selection of the proper inputs and outputs is controlled by the coincidence of the device address signals and the function pulses that are generated by the computer control circuitry. In this case, the device addresses 000 and 001 have been assigned to the UART. The function pulses $\overline{\text{IN}}$ (I/O READ) and $\overline{\text{OUT}}$ (I/O WRITE) are used to control the devices that are to apply data onto the data bus lines, or to accept data from the bus lines. In this way, even though the UART is a hardware circuit, it may be completely controlled by the proper use of software commands in the UART control program.

BUGBOOK® is a registered trademark of E & L Instruments, Inc., Derby, Connecticut 06418.

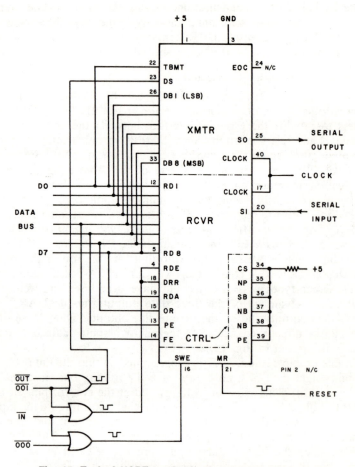

**Fig. 15. Typical UART-to-8080A microcomputer interface
(device decoders not shown for clarity).**

The software commands that are used to control the UART are:

IN   000   Input the status bits into the A register of the 8080A.

                Bit D0   Transmitter Buffer Empty (TBMT) flag
                Bit D1   Not used
                Bit D2   Not used
                Bit D3   Not used
                Bit D4   Framing Error (FE) flag
                Bit D5   Parity Error (PE) flag
                Bit D6   Overrun Error (OR) flag
                Bit D7   Received Data Available (RDA) flag

IN   001   Input the 8-bit data word from the receiver section into the 8080A A register and clear the Received Data Available (RDA) flag.

OUT   001   Output the 8-bit data word from the 8080A A register to the UART transmitter and initiate the transmission.

Simple programs may be written to control the flow of data to and from the computer and a teletypewriter or terminal to which the UART is connected. An example of a simple teletypewriter output program is shown in Fig. 16, and an example of a simple input program is shown in Fig. 17.

In the teletypewriter output program, Fig. 16, we have assumed that the 8-bit character code that was to be output to the teletypewriter was already present in the A register or accumulator of the 8080A. We have also assumed that the character to be printed was in the proper format, i.e., ASCII, EDCDIC, etc. The TTYOUT program places the computer in a loop in which the transmitter buffer flag is constantly checked until the buffer is found to be empty. When the flag indicates the empty condition, the character is transferred from the 8080A to the UART Transmitter Buffer Register to await transmission. After this transfer is completed, the TTYOUT subroutine returns control to the main program that called the subroutine.

The TTYIN subroutine, shown in Fig. 17, also waits for the appropriate flag, the Received Data Available flag. When this flag signals that a data word has been received, the software steps transfer the data word from the UART three-state receiver outputs to the 8080A accumulator. The input program that we have provided in Fig. 17 does not check the state of the three error flags, although steps could be readily added to do this. In most cases, these flags are ignored and we have not felt the need to include this error-checking in any of our programs.

```
TTYOUT,  PUSHPSW  /TEMPORARILY STORE REG A
LOOP,    IN       /INPUT STATUS BITS
         000
         ANI      /MASK OUT ALL BUT THE
         001      /TBMT FLAG
         JZ       /IF ZERO (NOT READY) CHECK
         LOOP     /IT AGAIN, SO GO BACK TO
         0        /LOOP
         POPPSW   /GET THE DATA BACK FROM THE STACK
         OUT      /OUTPUT IT TO THE UART
         001
         RET      /RETURN TO THE CALLING PROGRAM
```

Fig. 16. Simple UART output program for 8080-based computer.

```
TTYIN,    IN       /INPUT THE STATUS BITS
          000
          ANI      /MASK OUT ALL BUT THE
          200      /RDA FLAG
          JZ       /IF NOT SET, CHECK AGAIN
          TTYIN
          0
          IN       /RDA FLAG DETECTED, SO INPUT
          001      /THE DATA THEN
          RET      /RETURN
```

Fig. 17. Simple UART input program for 8080-based computer.

One note of caution is needed. The outputs of the receiver section and the flag outputs, while they are three-state and compatible with the signal levels on the microcomputer bus lines, *may require a long period to go from the third state to the "data state,"* and thus, they may be *incompatible with the computer timing requirements.* The UART three-state outputs may require as much as 250 nanoseconds to respond to the commands to place the receiver or flag data on the data bus. This is probably a short enough period so that most computer systems would not expect the data sooner, *but some UART chips have even slower access times.*

If the UART that you are planning to use with your microcomputer does not have a fast enough access time, there are two solutions that may be implemented. These are: (1) replace the UART with one that can "keep up" with the computer, or (2) permanently enable the three-state outputs and place sets of three-state buffers between the receiver outputs and the data bus and between the flag outputs and the data bus. These three-state buffers would then be enabled to transfer the data to the bus. We have had to do this in several cases.

A typical UART-based communication interface is shown in Fig. 18. In this example, the clocks, extra three-state buffers, and driver circuits have all been incorporated on the same printed-circuit board.

The software examples that we have provided in Figs. 16 and 17 are useful in themselves, but we recommend *8080/8085 Software Design* (Howard W. Sams & Co., Inc., Indianapolis, IN 46206, 1978) if you would like to know more about the use of software to control external devices.

Microcomputer—USART Interfacing

As you probably noticed in the previous section, there were many multiple data bus connections between the UART and the microcomputer data bus. When the UART concept was adapted for use in a more general-purpose communication integrated circuit, these multiple, parallel connections and others were combined within the new chips so that only a single set of eight connections were needed between the chip and the microcomputer data bus. Many of the functions were combined within the chip to simplify the interfacing task. As always, this presented a trade-off situation. As the hardware connections were simplified, additional software steps were required to properly control the new communication interface chips. In general, microcomputer families have their own bus- and signal-compatible communication chips, but some of these new chips have been designed so that they are readily interfaced to many of the various popular microcomputer chips.

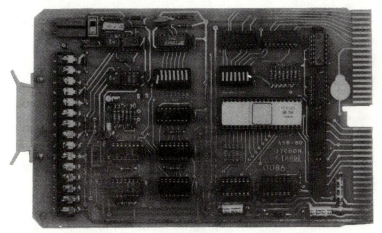

Fig. 18. Typical UART-based microcomputer-terminal interface card (drivers, buffers, and clock circuits contained on this single board).

In this section, we will describe the operation of the 8080A-compatible Universal Synchronous-Asynchronous Receiver/Transmitter, or USART, the Intel 8251A integrated circuit. We will not be concerned with the synchronous mode of data transmission/reception, since this is generally not used in small systems; and in any case, it is beyond the scope of this book. A block diagram of the USART chip and its pin configuration are shown in Fig. 19.

The USART chip contains the expected transmitter and receiver sections, but since it must be controlled by a microcomputer, some internal control logic is included. A data bus buffer provides an interface between the USART internal data bus and the microcomputer data bus lines. An additional MODEM control section is also provided. We shall discuss this section later. You will probably note that there are fewer pins on the USART package (28 pins) than

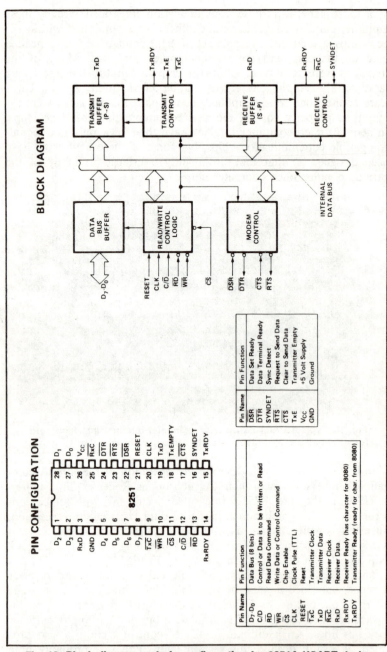

Fig. 19. Block diagram and pin configuration for 8251A USART device (reprinted by permission of Intel Corporation, Copyright 1978).

there are on the UART package (40 pins). There are no pins on the USART for programming the number of stop bits, parity, etc. Likewise, there are no error flags present as output pins on the USART package. These functions are controlled and tested through the use of control registers that are internal to the USART chip, and through the use of software instructions.

At this point, the most important signals for us to examine are those associated with the read/write control logic and the data bus. The CLK or clock input, pin 20, is generally derived from the 8080A microcomputer clock signal generator, an 8224 chip, or equivalent circuitry, or in the case of the 8085 microcomputer, derived from the clock output available from the 8085 chip itself. This clock must operate at a frequency that is at least 30 times faster than the fastest bit rate expected. This clock signal is used for internal control functions and *it is not used as either the transmitter or the receiver clock signal.*

When the USART Reset input, pin 21, goes to a logic one, the USART is reset. The reset pulse must be at least six clock periods long to allow the internal reset functions to take place. The clock periods are referenced to the general USART clock input and not to either the receiver or the transmitter clock signal. The chip select input, $\overline{CS}$, pin 11, is used to select the chip for operation, i.e., for all operations involving the transfer of data between the microcomputer and the USART. *The chip select does not affect the receiver or the transmitter as far as the transfer of serial data is concerned.* These functions are independent of the state of the chip select input signal.

The USART Read input, $\overline{RD}$, pin 13 and Write input, $\overline{WR}$, pin 10, are used by the microcomputer to control the flow of data to (write operation) and from (read operation) the USART and the microcomputer. While the USART chip may be used in a number of configurations, we have chosen to show it in the accumulator I/O mode. Thus, the USART signals are connected, $\overline{RD}$ to $\overline{IN}$ and $\overline{WR}$ to $\overline{OUT}$. The $\overline{IN}$ and $\overline{OUT}$ signals are generated by the 8080A microcomputer control logic and they are often called $\overline{I/O\ READ}$ and $\overline{I/O\ WRITE}$, as noted previously.

The Command/Data input, C/D, pin 12, is used by the 8080A to indicate to the USART chip the kinds of data that are being transferred to it, or requested from it. This information can consist of commands that are used to reconfigure the USART, or it can be data for transmission. When the C/D signal is a logic one, commands are transferred, and when it is a logic zero, eight bits of data are transferred between the USART and the microcomputer. The read and write signals are used by the microcomputer to signal the USART as to the direction of data flow on the 8-bit data bus. In all cases, if data are to be transferred between the chips, the chip select input must be in the logic zero state.

The C/D input is generally wired to the least significant address bit of the 8080A, A0, so that there are two device addresses associated with each USART chip. X and X+1, of, for example, 10100000 and 10100001. The most significant seven address bits do not change and they are generally decoded with some additional circuitry to provide the chip select signal that enables the USART.

The truth table shown in Fig. 20 shows the relationship between the control inputs and the USART functions.

Signal Conditions				Function
$\overline{CS}$	$\overline{WR}$	$\overline{RD}$	C/D	
0	1	0	0	Read the USART Status
0	0	1	0	Write Mode/Command
0	1	0	1	Read Received Data
0	0	1	1	Write Transmit Data
1	X	X	X	USART Not Selected
X = Don't care condition, logic one or logic zero				

Fig. 20. Truth Table for USART control inputs.

The USART status "word" is used to indicate to the 8080A what the status of the receiver and the transmitter is, while the Command/Mode word is used by the computer to control the operation of the USART. These "words" will be examined in detail. A typical 8080A-USART interface is shown in Fig. 21. Only the microcomputer-to-USART interconnections have been shown for clarity. Note that the device address 240 (ADDR 240) should not include bit A0 in its decoding scheme.

The USART is controlled in its asynchronous mode through the use of two control words: (1) a Mode Instruction word that formats the USART, and (2) a Command Instruction that actually controls the USART operation. The format of the Mode Instruction is shown in Fig. 22. Through the proper selection of the bits, the USART may be programmed for various kinds of data, with different parity, stop bits, and character-length formats. These individual bits in the Mode Instruction are used to replace the individual programming pins that are found on a UART chip. Since we will not be discussing the USART synchronous mode, Bits B1 and B2 cannot both be zero. The Mode Instruction also allows a "baud-rate factor" to be selected. This is the multiple of the bit rate at which the transmitter and receiver clocks must operate. In our example, we will use a factor of 16; the clock must be set so that its frequency is 16 times the bit-rate frequency. Thus, for a rate of 1200 bits per second, the receiver and transmitter clock must be 18.2 kHz.

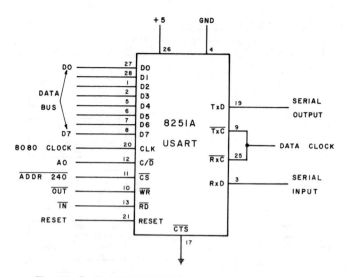

Fig. 21. Typical USART-8080A microcomputer interface
(unused connections are not shown).

The Mode Instruction word, 11101110 is used to configure the
USART for the following mode of operation:

(a) Two stop bits
(b) No parity, even parity overridden

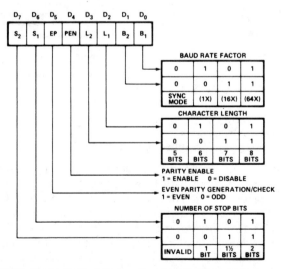

Fig. 22. 8251A Mode Control Instruction format for asynchronous mode
(reprinted by permission of Intel Corporation, Copyright 1978).

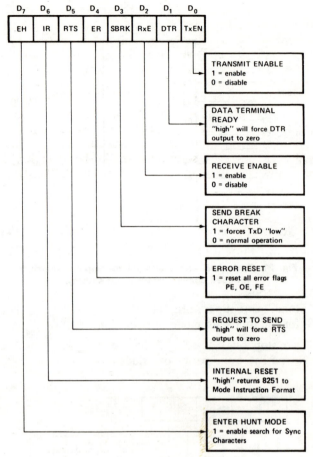

Fig. 23. 8251A Command Instruction format (reprinted by permission of Intel Corporation, Copyright 1978).

(c) Eight bits of data

(d) A clock rate 16 times the bit rate

Immediately after the Mode Instruction word has been transferred from the 8080A to the USART, by writing it out to port 241, a Command Instruction word must also be loaded into the USART. *In fact, the Command Instruction word is also written to output port 241. The USART internal logic directs the Mode and Command Instructions to their proper registers within the USART chip.* The format of the Command Instruction word is shown in Fig. 23. We shall not be concerned with some of the bits in the command instruction, since their use will not affect the asynchronous mode of operation.

We will be mainly interested in the Transmit Enable bit, D0, and the Receive Enable bit, D2.

The word 00000101 may be used as the Command Instruction word to enable both the transmitter and receiver. In any case, *the Mode Instruction word must be output to the USART first, followed by the Command Instruction word.* If the USART is reset, a new Mode/Command Instruction output sequence must be generated by the computer. The Command Instruction may be changed at any time simply by sending the USART a new Command Instruction word. The Mode Instruction may also be changed, but a reset is needed to do this. The software example shown in Fig. 24 may be used to load the two 8-bit instructions into the USART in the proper order.

Note that the Command Instruction can be used to generate an internal reset condition so that a new Mode Instruction can be configured and transferred to the USART. However, a reset pulse is still required whenever power is re-applied to the microcomputer system.

```
USART,   MVI A      /LOAD REG A WITH MODE INSTR
         356        /356 = 11101110
         OUT        /OUTPUT IT TO THE USART
         241
         MVI A      /LOAD REG A WITH COMMAND INSTR
         005        /005 = 00000101
         OUT        /OUTPUT IT TO THE USART
         241
         NOP        /PROGRAM CONTINUES HERE
```

Fig. 24. Software steps used to initialize USART for eight data bits, no parity, and two stop bits.

Once the USART has been initialized with the proper Mode and Command instructions, the USART may be used to transmit and receive data. In our interfacing example (Fig. 21), the receiver data are available at input port 240 and the data that are to be transmitted are output to output port 240. When the computer reads data from input port 241, the USART status bits are read into the A register. These bits are used to indicate the status of the various USART functions. The format of the Status Word is shown in Fig. 25. Three of the status bits are used to indicate error conditions, as did the outputs of the flags with the same names on the UART chip. You should be familiar with these error flags. The SYNDET bit is not used in the asynchronous mode.

The important bits in the asynchronous mode are the RxRDY (receiver ready, bit D1) and TxRDY (transmitter ready, bit D0)

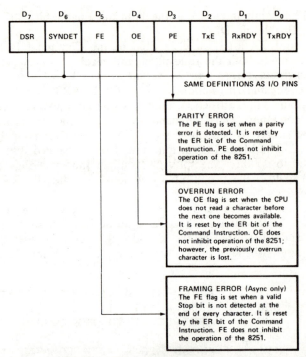

Fig. 25. The USART Status Word bit assignments—TxRDY and RxRDY flags are the important ones (reprinted by permission of Intel Corporation, Copyright 1978).

bits or flags. The RxRDY bit indicates that the receiver has a data word ready for the computer. The RxRDY flag is automatically reset during the data-read operation, in which the received data word is transferred to the 8080A microcomputer. The UART, you may remember, required a separate signal for this flag-resetting operation. The TxRDY bit indicates that the transmitter section is ready to accept the next data word for transmission. The TxEMPTY (transmitter empty, bit D2) flag indicates that the transmitter has completed its transmissions and that it is in the idle state.

A typical USART teletypewriter input program is shown in Fig. 26; a teletypewriter output program is shown in Fig. 27.

Note that in the TTYIN subroutine, the received character is left in the A register of the 8080A at the end of the subroutine. The TTYOUT subroutine expects that the A register contains the value that is to be transmitted.

The TxRDY, RxRDY and TxEMPTY flags have corresponding output pins on the USART chip so that these flags may also be used for other purposes. The TxD and RxD pins are the Transmitter

```
TTYIN,    IN         /INPUT THE USART'S STATUS BITS
          241
          ANI        /MASK ALL BUT THE
          002        /RXRDY BIT
          JZ         /IF NOT READY, CHECK AGAIN
          TTYIN
          0
          IN         /READY, SO GET THE DATA BITS
          240
          RET        /RETURN WITH DATA IN REG A
```

Fig. 26. Typical USART input subroutine (data are
input into the 8080A's A register).

serial data output and the Receiver serial data input pins, respectively. The $\overline{\text{TxC}}$ and $\overline{\text{RxC}}$ pins are the respective clock inputs for the transmitter and receiver sections. These are the clock signals that govern the data-bit rates. It is important that you not confuse these signals with the general-purpose clock input, CLK, that is used for internal control functions. The USART receiver and transmitter may have different data rates, but, as was the case with the UART, the data formats of both must be the same.

Modem Control

While it is not our purpose here to discuss the actual control of a modem or modulator/demodulator circuit, there are several pins on the USART that can be used for this purpose. These are:

$\overline{\text{DSR}}$	Data Set Ready	(pin 22)	(Input)
$\overline{\text{CTS}}$	Clear to Send	(pin 17)	(Input)
$\overline{\text{DTR}}$	Data Terminal Ready	(pin 24)	(Output)
$\overline{\text{RTS}}$	Request to Send	(pin 23)	(Output)

```
TTYOUT,   PUSHPSW    /SAVE REG A ON THE STACK
TEST,     IN         /INPUT THE USART'S STATUS BITS
          241
          ANI        /MASK ALL BUT THE
          001        /TXRDY BIT
          JZ         /IF NOT READY, TEST IT AGAIN
          TEST
          0
          POPPSW     /GET REG A BACK OFF THE STACK
          OUT        /OUTPUT THE DATA TO THE USART
          240
          RET        /RETURN
```

Fig. 27. Typical USART output subroutine (code to be
transmitted must be placed in A register).

For the normal operation of the USART transmitter, the $\overline{CTS}$ input must be a logic zero. If it is not a logic zero, the transmitter will be disabled. The TxEN bit in the Command Instruction must also be used to enable the transmitter. If you are not going to use the USART with a modem, we suggest that you ground the $\overline{CTS}$ pin, pin 17.

While the three remaining signals may be used for modem control, they may also be used for other purposes, such as the control of an audio cassette or paper tape reader. The Data Set Ready input may be tested by the computer as bit D7 in the Status Word. Perhaps this could be used with an external switch to indicate to the computer that it is connected to a local terminal or to a remote data acquisition system. In this way, the computer would be able to determine with which device it was communicating. The two outputs, Data Terminal Ready and Request to Send. mav be set and reset through the use of bits D1 and D5, respectively, in the Command Instruction word. These outputs provide the computer with two additional control outputs that are directly controlled by software. A complete data sheet for the USART device is provided in the appendix.

Other USART-like Communication Interface Chips

Most families of microcomputers have some form of asynchronous serial interface chip. The Motorola 6800-series microcomputer uses an MC6850 Asynchronous Communications Interface Adapter (ACIA). The Zilog Z-80 uses the Z-80 SIO (serial I/O) chip, and so on. Many of the newer chips also support other "protocols" of serial data exchange, such as synchronous, synchronous data link control (SDLC), and others.

The National Semiconductor Corporation's INS8250 UART device is compatible with microcomputers; it has the ability to allow the microcomputer to select the actual bit rate to be used for data transfers.

The Programmable Communication Interface (PCI) 2651 by Signetics Corporation is very similar to the Intel 8251A in its operation. *However, it is not a pin-for-pin replacement.* The 2651 has an additional Mode Instruction register that allows for the selection of the actual bit rate that will be used with the device. Several clock options are available. The clock signal may be generated by an external source, such as an oscillator, as per the UART and USART chips, or the clock signal may be generated internally. An internal clock may also be selected through the use of the additional Mode Instruction, but if the internal clock is used, both the transmitter and the receiver will operate at the same data rate. When a 5.0688-MHz clock signal is provided to the 2651, bit rates from 50 to 19,200 bits per second may be selected.

Portions of the Signetics 2651 integrated-circuit data sheet have been provided in the appendix. The sections provided are particularly useful, since they clearly show the designations of the individual bits in each register. The 2651 may also be used in the synchronous mode.

Undoubtedly, there will be additional communication chips introduced by the various integrated-circuit manufacturers in the years to come. You should still be able to find that a basic understanding of the UART chip is extremely useful in understanding the operation of these new devices.

Current Loops and Voltage Signals

In previous sections, you have probably realized that when the TTL-compatible logic families are used, a 0-volt signal represented a logic zero and a 3- to 5-volt signal represented a logic one. Since it is generally not good digital design practice to transmit these TTL-level signals over a distance of more than 10 inches, they generally are not used for long-distance serial data communications. Most asynchronous serial teletypewriters and terminals use one of two popular serial communication interface standards, either the 20-milliampere current loop, or the Electronic Industry Association's RS-232C standard voltage levels. In this section, we shall discuss both of these standards and how these signals are translated into the logic levels that are required to drive the UART and USART devices.

20-Milliampere Current Loops

Current loops use low-impedance transmission lines that are resistant to noise. Typically, these lines are twisted pairs of wires. The Teletype Corporation Model ASR-33 teletypewriter is a good example of a device that communicates over a 20-mA current loop. The conventions for the logic states in a current loop are:

Logic 1 = Current of about 20 mA flowing in the loop.
Logic 0 = Current of between 0 and 2 mA flowing in the loop.

Most current loops can be used to communicate between devices that are located some distance from the transmitter or receiver. A schematic diagram of a typical current loop is shown in Fig. 28. As you examine this figure, note the following:

- The 20-mA current flowing in the loop is generated by a 15-volt source and a 20-mA current regulator. The regulator may be a series resistor or a slightly more complex circuit. We recommend a series voltage source of at least 12 volts for use in current loops.

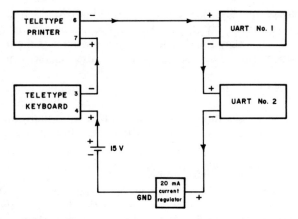

Fig. 28. Typical current loop for teletypewriter-UART interface.

- One or more UARTs may be tied to the loop. The serial input
  and output of the UART must have 20-mA current converters
  connected to them. The standard TTL-level signals *cannot* be
  used directly in the loop.

The teletypewriter connections have been shown with numbers
that represent the connections on the internal barrier terminal strip

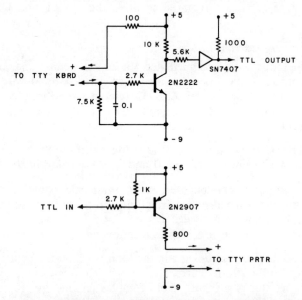

Fig. 29. Typical 20 mA/TTL interface circuits (circuits supply
own voltage source and current for loops).

of the teletypewriter. The teletypewriter must be set for 20-mA operation. The printer is often called the *receiver,* since it receives and prints the characters. The keyboard is the *transmitter,* since it sends the character-codes to another device on the loop. Pay particular attention to the direction that the current flows in the loop.

There are many circuits that can be used to convert the TTL-compatible signals into the 20-mA current levels, and to convert the 20-mA current levels back into the TTL-compatible voltages required by the UARTs. Two typical circuits are shown in Fig. 29. In each case, the current has been produced through a series resistor in the current loop, rather than through a current regulator circuit. Converter circuits, such as those shown in Fig. 29, may be used when the teletypewriter or terminal is not too far from the converter circuits. These circuits are not recommended when the terminal device is some distance from the converter circuits. Note that the current loop is not *isolated* from the converter and that noise picked up on the current loop lines can be transmitted back into the logic circuits. When an isolated current loop is used, the electrical circuit that provides the current for the loop will be isolated from the other circuitry. Thus, there will be no electrical connections between the current loop and the logic circuits.

When actual isolation of the current loop from the computer or other circuitry is required, optical couplers or optical isolators are very frequently used. Typical transmitters and receiver circuits are shown in Fig. 30. In each case, a separate 20-mA current sink/source is required. A typical 20-mA current sink circuit is shown in Fig. 31.

The optical couplers are used to electrically isolate the computer and UART circuit from the current loop. One signal is converted to a low-level light output from a light-emitting diode. The light is channeled to a sensitive phototransistor which reconverts the light to an electrical signal that is amplified and used elsewhere. Thus, there is no direct electrical connection between the light-emitting diode and the phototransistor. Voltage isolation of up to 30,000 volts is possible, although the isolation in the 4N35 optical coupler, shown in Fig. 30, is approximately 1500 volts. Optical couplers are also frequently used to switch loads that could not normally be switched by using a direct electrical connection between the switching circuit and the load itself.

To speed your interfacing task, we have developed the LR-14 TTL/20-mA Current Loop Interface Outboard module. This module contains a TTL-to-20 mA converter, a 20 mA-to-TTL converter, and a 20-mA current sink. A photograph of an LR-14 module is shown in Fig. 32. The circuits used have been shown previously in Figs. 30 and 31. The specifications for the LR-14 module are as follows:

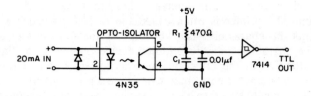

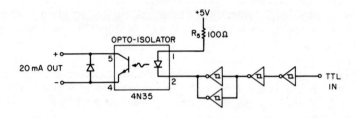

Fig. 30. Typical 20-mA current/TTL converter circuit uses optical coupler (circuits require voltage source and current regulator).

- TTL Input: Fan-in of one.
- TTL Output: Fan-out of 10.
- Current loop: Logic zero—Less than 3-mA current.
  Logic one—More than 15-mA current.
  The maximum loop source voltage is 30 volts.
- On-board optical isolation of current loops and logic signals.

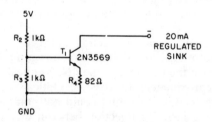

Fig. 31. Circuit diagram for 20-mA current sink (usually used with +12- to +30-volt source).

Fig. 32. LR-14 Outboard module for TTL/20-mA current loop conversions.

- On-board 20-mA regulated current sink. This "sink" is not isolated from the logic circuitry and it should not be used if complete electrical isolation of the current loop and logic circuits is required.
- Data transmission rates: 20 kbits/second minimum
  30 kbits/second typical
  40 kbits/second maximum
- An on-board provision for a filter capacitor that may be added to increase the noise immunity of the system. A 0.01-microfarad capacitor is provided so that the system may be operated at the maximum data rate. The *maximum* data transmission rates for various *added* capacitances are shown below.

Capacitance (μf)	Transmission Rates
1	0 to 300 b/sec*
0.5	0 to 1 kb/sec
0.1	0 to 10 kb/sec
0.05	0 to 15 kb/sec
None	0 to 20 kb/sec

* Teletypewriter operation range.

Voltage Signals

Some asynchronous-serial–based devices use voltage levels rather than current to communicate with computers, instruments, etc. Clearly, these voltage signals cannot be standard TTL voltages found in digital systems. Most serial devices that use voltage levels use the EIA RS-232C standard voltage levels. These may be summarized as:

Logic 1 = Voltage between −5 and −15 volts.
Logic 0 = Voltage between +5 and +15 volts.

There are many integrated circuits that may be used to receive and generate these levels, translating them to and from the standard TTL-compatible voltage levels. The Signetics Corporation 8T15 and 8T16 devices are typical examples. The pin configurations for these integrated circuits are shown in Fig. 33. When properly used, these devices will drive long communication lines.

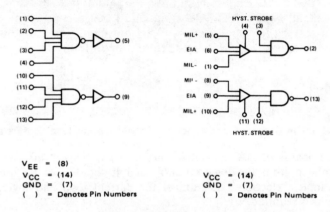

**Fig. 33. Functional diagrams and pin assignments
for 8T15 and 8T16 integrated circuits.**

For the 8T15 Line Driver integrated circuit, the V_{cc} voltage may be between +12 and +15 volts and the V_{ee} voltage may be between −12 and −15 volts. We prefer the +12 and −12 volt supplies. The V_{cc} voltage for the 8T16 Line Receiver is typically +5 volts, so that its logic output is compatible with TTL circuits. The 8T16 has about 4 volts of noise immunity, so it can reject a great deal of noise that may be induced on the electrical signal that it is receiving.

To aid in interfacing RS-232C-compatible signals to standard TTL devices, we have developed the LR-13 Line Driver/Receiver RS232 Outboard® module. This module contains one of the 8T15 and one of the 8T16 circuits. The specifications for the LR-13 Outboard module are as follows:

Each driver on the 8T15 performs the logical AND function for four inputs and it will accept standard TTL levels. The output is buffered to drive interface lines with nominal voltage levels of +6 and −6 volts. The outputs are protected against damage caused by accidental shorting to a potential as great as ±25 volts. The driver circuit that is connected to pins 1 through 5 is used as the TTL-to-RS232C interface. The other driver in the integrated circuit, connected to pins 9 through 13 is available for other applications. The pins of this second circuit are available on the rear of the Outboard module.

The 8T16 Line Receiver accepts either single-ended or differential signals and converts them to standard TTL levels. The receiver at pins 9 through 13 is used as the RS-232C-to-TTL interface. The other receiver, connected to pins 1 through 6, is available for other applications. The pins of this second circuit are available at the rear of the Outboard module. When using the EIA input, both of the MIL inputs must be grounded. The EIA input may be left unconnected if it is not used. The strobe input must be a logic one to allow data to pass through the device. If the strobe input is a logic zero, the output will be in the logic one state and data will not be passed through the device.

Fig. 34. LR-13 Outboard module for RS-232C/TTL conversions.

The LR-13 Outboard module is shown in Fig. 34. A 16-pin integrated-circuit socket has been used at the rear of the module to allow connections to be readily made to the unused circuitry in each of the integrated-circuit converter chips used.

The Teletypewriter

The Model Automatic Send/Receive-33 teletypewriter (ASR-33) manufactured by the Teletype Corporation, Skokie, IL 60076, is basically a typewriter that communicates via a set of asynchronous serial characters sent over a 20-mA current loop. The ASR-33 teletypewriter shown in Fig. 35 contains a keyboard, a printer mechanism, a paper tape punch and a paper tape reader. Rather than develop our own description of the teletypewriter, we provide you with several paragraphs through the courtesy of the Digital Equipment Corporation *PDP-8E and PDP-8M small Computer Handbook,* copyright 1971, Digital Equipment Corporation, Maynard, MA. These are given in Tables 2 and 3.

Fig. 35. Top view of keyboard and printer of ASR-33 teletypewriter.

The most important control on the teletypewriter is the LINE/ OFF/LOCAL switch that controls the entire teletypewriter. In the LINE position, the teletypewriter is connected to the asynchronous serial data transmission line and it is thus connected to the 20-mA current loops. In the LOCAL position, the connections to the 20-mA current loops are disconnected, but the teletypewriter acts as a typewriter. Asynchronous serial signals are not generated, nor received. In the OFF position, the mechanism does not respond to any operation. Note that even when the teletype is placed in the off state, some of the internal circuitry of the teletypewriter still draws power from the 110 vac line power, so it should be unplugged if it will not be used for some time.

A complete chart of all of the ASCII characters and their equivalent codes is provided in the appendix. Since most teletypewriters,

Table 2. ASR Teletypewriter Controls and Functions

CONTROL or INDICATOR	FUNCTION
REL Pushbutton	Disengages the paper tape in the punch to allow for tape loading or removal.
B SP Pushbutton	Backspaces the paper tape in the punch by one space, allowing for manual correction or rubout of the character just punched.
ON/OFF Pushbutton	Controls the use of the paper tape punch with operation of the teletypewriter's keyboard/printer.
START/STOP/FREE Switch	Controls the use of the paper tape reader with operation of the teletypewriter. In the FREE position, the reader is disengaged, permitting the tape to be moved manually within the reader without necessarily reloading or unloading it. In the STOP position, the reader mechanism is engaged, but de-energized. In the START position, the reader is engaged and operated under program control. The tape may be either loaded or unloaded in the FREE or STOP modes.
Keyboard	Provides a means of printing on paper and punching on paper tape when in the LOCAL mode and of transmitting data to and receiving data from a computer or remote device when in the LINE mode.
LINE/OFF/LOCAL Switch	Controls the application of power to the teletypewriter and the data connections to the computer. In the LINE position, the teletypewriter is energized and connected to the computer or other asynchronous serial device. In the OFF position, the teletypewriter is off. In the LOCAL position, the teletypewriter is energized, but the connections to external devices are broken, and the teletypewriter functions as a typewriter.

Keyboard Operation

The teletypewriter keyboard is similar to a typewriter keyboard, except that some nonprinting characters are included on the key tops. Top typing symbols such as, $, %, and #, which appear on the upper portion of the numeric keys and certain of the alphabetic keys, the SHIFT key is depressed while the desired key is actuated.

Designations for certain nonprinting functions are also shown on the upper portion of certain of the keys. By depressing the CTRL (control) key and then depressing the desired key, these control functions are actuated and their corresponding code transmitted. The information in Table 3 lists keys that have useful functions that are applicable to many computer systems.

Table 3. Special Teletypewriter Keyboard Functions

KEY	FUNCTION	USE
SPACE	Space	Used to combine and delimit (separate) symbols and numbers in computer programs.
RETURN	Carriage Return	Used to terminate the entry of a line of data or a line of a program. Returns the printing element to the left-hand margin.
LINE FEED	Line Feed	Advances the printer to the next line on the paper. Generally used in conjunction with the carriage return to provide a clean line for the next series of data or program entries.
RUBOUT	Rubout	Used by many computer programs to delete the last character entered. This allows for error correction.
HERE IS	Blank tape	The HERE IS key may be used when the teletypewriter is in the LOCAL mode with the paper tape punch ON to generate several inches of blank, unpunched tape.
CTRL/REPT/P	Code 200_8	Used with the paper tape punch in the LOCAL mode to generate "trailer" and "leader" sections on a paper tape. These sections are often used by computers to detect the start and the end of programs and data that are stored on punched paper tape.

Printer Operation

The printer mechanism provides a typed copy (hard copy) of input and output at a rate of 10 characters per second. When the teletypewriter is in the LINE mode, the data that are transmitted to the printer are printed. In the LOCAL mode, the data typed on the keyboard are reproduced on the printer.

Paper Tape Reader Operation

The paper tape reader is used to transmit data, messages or computer programs that have been previously punched onto paper tape. The eight-channel (eight punched holes per column) paper tape is read at the rate of ten characters per second. The reader's controls are:

START Activates the reader and engages the sprocket wheel to read the punched paper tape

STOP Deactivates (stops) the reader, but the sprocket wheel is engaged and the tape cannot be manually moved.

FREE The reader is deactivated and the paper tape sprocket moves freely, allowing the tape to be manually pulled through the reader. The tape is not read when this is done.

and some terminals, do not have the capacity to print, or display, the lower-case alphabet characters, only the upper-case letters can be transmitted and received. Some of the ASCII characters are not used in this case and this abbreviated ASCII character set is often called the "half-ASCII" code. We will not use this term, but you may hear it from time to time.

INTRODUCTION TO THE EXPERIMENTS

In the experiments that follow, you will wire and test a variety of circuits in which the Universal Asynchronous Receiver/Transmitter (UART) is used to receive and transmit data. The use of 20-milliampere current loops will also be explored, as will their interaction with a teletypewriter. It is our hope that you will better understand the functioning of the UART chip once you have completed these experiments.

In many cases these days, people are interested in using UARTs and their computer-based counterparts, Universal Synchronous/Asynchronous Receiver/Transmitters (USARTs) in computer applications. It is very difficult to breadboard and test many of these devices, since they must be controlled by a microcomputer. Since most of the UART-like functions are incorporated in these newer chips, we feel that a thorough understanding of the UART itself will better help you understand the operation of these newer devices. Therefore, we encourage you to do, or at least read through, these experiments.

We have developed the LR-21 UART Outboard® module so that you can readily and easily wire the UART circuits shown in these experiments. If you choose to use the LR-21 Outboard module, we suggest that you use a flexible flat cable with 16-pin dual in-line headers at each end. This will allow you to quickly connect the LR-21 Outboard module to the eight lamp monitors and switches that are used. The cables and headers are flexible and fragile, so we suggest that you carefully press the pins into a piece of Styrofoam when they are not in use.

The LR-21 Outboard module is shown in Fig. 36. In this picture, a CMOS UART chip is shown in the socket.

It is easy to connect the receiver and transmitter bits in the reverse order. Check these connections carefully. You should also be sure to reset the UART whenever power is re-applied to the chip. You may do this with a wire jumper, or a pulser may be used. We have favored the use of a jumper. You can quickly reset the UART by taking pin 21, RESET, to a logic one and then back to the logic zero state.

If you plan to use a set of batteries to obtain the −12 volts required by the PMOS UART chips, be sure that the battery, or bat-

Fig. 36. Top view of LR-21 UART Outboard module showing program and receiver/transmitter data plugs (CMOS UART is shown).

teries, are connected properly and that there is a good common ground between the battery and the UART circuit.

The Intersil or Harris CMOS UART chips may be used in these experiments. There are some differences between these CMOS devices and the usual PMOS UART chips. These include:

- The CMOS chip requires the +5-volt supply. **DO NOT** connect a CMOS UART to the −12-volt power supply. This will destroy it. We recommend the use of the IM6402 UART chip, if you wish to use a CMOS UART device. The IM6403 device has so many differences that it would prove difficult to use in these experiments, particularly if you are not familiar with the UART-type chips.
- The inputs to a CMOS UART may not be left unconnected to simulate the logic one condition. They must be connected to the +5-volt power supply through 10-kilohm resistors to generate the logic one condition.
- While the CMOS UART may have various power supplies connected to it, we recommend the use of the +5-volt power supply so that the inputs and outputs are TTL-compatible.

In many of the experiments, seven-segment displays have been shown. These have been used for the display of the UART receiver data in the octal format. You may wish to substitute lamp monitors for these displays so that each output has its own light-emitting diode. The lamp monitors are less expensive than the seven-segment displays and their outputs will display the more general binary code.

The fan-out (output drive capability) of the UARTs is limited, so that one UART output will typically drive a single TTL input (SN7400 series). Thus, if one of the UART outputs is required in more than one place, a buffer of some kind is required. We have shown an SN7408 buffer used for this purpose. Only one SN7408 integrated circuit is used; however, equivalent circuits may work just as well.

In some of the schematic diagrams you will notice a "0" or a "1" next to a pin designation. This indicates that this pin must be placed at a logic zero or at a logic one, respectively, for the chip to operate properly. We have used the designations, "0" and "1" to distinguish these logical connections from the current-carrying power connections to the chips.

We found that a logic probe was very helpful in troubleshooting the UART circuits. Actually, the circuit is relatively simple, but when you are troubleshooting 30 of them in a classroom, the logic probe is very helpful. An oscilloscope or a digital frequency meter is useful in tuning up the UART clock frequencies. The oscilloscope is also useful if you wish to examine the UART serial output at data transmission speeds such that a lamp monitor is no longer useful.

A typical experimental breadboard is shown in Fig. 37. A 6-volt lantern battery has been used to supply the voltage for both the logic integrated circuits and also for the UART. One of the newer, single-supply UARTs has been used in this set-up. In some experiments, more than one solderless breadboard may be required.

If you will be using the LR-21 UART Outboard module in your experiments, we recommend that you carefully examine the overlay for the LR-21 Outboard module that has been reproduced in the

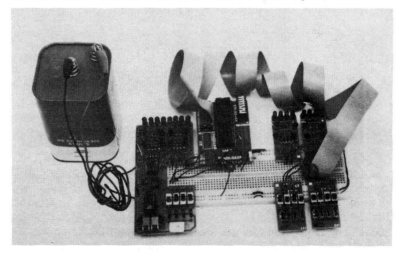

Fig. 37. Typical UART breadboard (Outboard modules used to simplify wiring—note use of flat cable to reduce interconnect wiring—single-supply UART is shown).

appendix, Fig. 50. This shows the locations of the data and control signals at the three dual-in-line sockets provided on the board. Some of the control signals are also provided at the edge of the card so that it is easily used with the solderless breadboards. A complete LR-21 Outboard module is shown in Fig. 36, with an experimental breadboard shown in Fig. 37. You may wish to refer to these figures as you set up your experiments.

The Outboard modules are available from E&L Instruments, Inc., 61 First Street, Derby, CT 06418. Solderless breadboards are available from E&L Instruments and from AP Products, Inc., P. O. Box 110, Painsville, OH 44077.

EXPERIMENT NO. 1

Purpose

The purpose of this experiment is to demonstrate how the UART may be used to transmit an 8-bit binary data word from the transmitter section to the receiver section of the chip. *Be sure that you save your circuit for use in Experiment No. 2 and the following experiments.*

Pin Configurations of Integrated Circuits (Fig. 38)

In this experiment, the UART integrated circuit will be used along with an SN7408 buffer chip. Only the pin configuration for the SN7408 chip has been shown in Fig. 38, for clarity. Be sure that you connect the SN7408 pin 14 to +5 volts and pin 7 to ground.

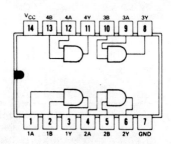

Fig. 38. Pin configuration of SN7408 quad two-input NAND gate buffer integrated circuit; +5 volts to pin 14 and ground to pin 7.

Schematic Diagram of Circuit (Fig. 39)

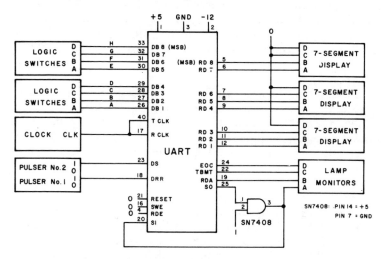

Fig. 39. Schematic diagram of basic UART circuit used in experiments (programming pins not shown for clarity).

Step 1

Study the schematic diagram carefully. You will note that the three error flags, Parity Error, Overrun and Framing Error, do not have their outputs used in this experiment. Likewise, the receiver/transmitter programming pins (pins 35 through 39) are not shown in the diagram.

Step 2

Wire the circuit shown in Fig. 39. As noted in the Introduction to the Experiments, you may wish to substitute lamp monitor Outboard modules for the seven-segment displays that are shown in Fig. 39. Be sure to include the SN7408 buffer circuit and its power connections.

You may find that two solderless breadboards are required for this experiment. We recommend that you use two breadboards so that the circuitry can be spread out. This will greatly aid in circuit check-out and in troubleshooting.

The programming pins of the UART should be wired to +5 volts or logic one. These are pins 35 through 39. The Control Strobe pin, pin 34, should also be wired to +5 volts to load the programming signals into the UART. These connections will program the UART for what type or format of data transmission?

The UART will be programmed for a transmission that will include a start bit, eight data bits, no parity bits and two stop bits. The parity selection has been overridden by the use of the no-parity option. Remember that the start bit cannot be "programmed." It is present in all asynchronous-serial–data transmissions from the UART.

Step 3

Set the logic switches HGFEDCBA to 00000001. Use a 0.05- or a 0.1-microfarad capacitor on the clock Outboard module, or with the equivalent clock circuitry. This will provide a relatively slow clock frequency, such as 10 Hz. Connect the power to the wired circuit. Be sure that the −12-volt power supply has also been connected to the UART chip. This is the *only* point at which −12 volts is required.

Whenever power is applied to the UART, it is generally necessary to reset it so that it will operate properly. To do this, simply remove the wire connecting the UART RESET input, pin 21 and ground. Momentarily connect pin 21 to logic one, or +5 volts to reset the UART. Now, reconnect the RESET pin, pin 21, and the ground bus on the solderless breadboard. Remember to do this whenever you remove and re-apply power to your UART circuit.

Press and release (actuate) Pulser No. 1, the pulser that is connected to the Data Ready Reset input. You should not observe any change on the lamp monitors, except that the Received Data Available (RDA) lamp monitor will go off, if it was on. Now press and release Pulser No. 2 connected to the UART Data Strobe input.

When Pulser No. 2 was pulsed did you observe any changes taking place at the lamp monitors that are attached to the UART End of Character (EOC), Transmitter Buffer Empty (TBMT), Received Data Available (RDA), and Serial Output (SO) pins? Was there a definite sequence of operation?

Can you explain the sequence of operation, i.e., the order in which the lamp monitors went from logic one to logic zero or vice versa?

We observed that all of the LEDs went off briefly. The Transmitter Buffer Empty flag LED came back on (logic one) quickly, since it took the UART very little time to transfer the 8-bit data word from the transmitter buffer register to the transmitter register for transmission. The logic one at the TBMT pin indicates that the UART transmitter buffer register could now be loaded with another data word. It would be transmitted right after the word that you first loaded.

The LED connected to the Serial Output will reflect the serial stream of bits that are being transmitted. If you are using a slow clock signal, you should allow up to 20 or 25 seconds to observe the serial data bits being transmitted and the final state of the lamp monitors.

The End of Character flag indicates that the UART has completed the transmission of the data. The Received Data Available flag indicates that the receiver has received the eight data bits and that they are available at the eight parallel outputs from the receiver section of the UART chip. You should also be able to observe that the Received Data Available (RDA) flag of the receiver becomes a logic one at the same time that the eight bits of data are available at the receiver outputs. If you are in doubt about this timing relationship, change the data bits that are set at the transmitter and transmit them to the receiver by actuating Pulser No. 2. Now observe the state of the RDA lamp monitor and the eight data outputs from the receiver section of the UART. You do not have to reset the Received Data Available flag each time that you transmit a new data word in this experiment, but unless you do so in this step, you will not be able to observe this timing relationship. Press and release Pulser No. 1 to do this.

Note, too, that the End of Character flag becomes a logic one *after* the data bits have been received. Why is this? Can you guess?

The End of Character flag indicates that the entire serial transmission has been completed, including the parity bit (if any) and the stop bit(s). The Received Data Available flag indicates that the eight bits have been received, it does not wait for the receipt of the stop bits.

Step 4

Change the eight data switches that are connected to the transmitter inputs. Transmit this new data word to the receiver. Remember that you have to actuate Pulser No. 2 to initiate the transmission. Do you observe the new 8-bit data word at the receiver outputs? Remember to wait for the completion of the transmission.

We did. Remember that if you are using the three seven-segment display Outboards, you will be reading the *octal* equivalents of the

8-bit binary codes. If you are using lamp monitors, you should be able to see a one-to-one correspondence between the eight inputs to the transmitter and the eight outputs from the receiver. Be sure that the wiring between the transmitter pins and the switches and between the receiver outputs and the displays is correct. It is often easy to "twist" a wire or to move one out of position.

Step 5

Replace the capacitor that you have been using with the clock with a capacitor that is 50 to 100 times smaller in value. We used a 0.001-microfarad capacitor in our circuit to generate a frequency of approximately 650 Hz. At such a frequency, it will take less than a second to transmit and receive an 8-bit data word.

Use the logic switch settings as shown in the following table. When the switch settings have been made on the switches connected to the transmitter, transmit the data to the receiver section of the UART and note your observations in the spaces provided. Space for the Octal (seven-segment) and Binary codes has been provided. Use either one.

Logic Switch Settings								Display Readings	
H	G	F	E	D	C	B	A	Octal	Binary
0	0	0	0	0	0	0	1		
0	1	0	0	1	0	0	1		
1	0	0	1	0	0	1	0		
1	1	0	1	1	0	1	1		
1	1	1	1	1	1	1	1		
1	0	1	1	0	0	0	0		
0	0	1	1	0	0	0	0		
0	1	0	1	0	1	0	1		

You do not have to reset the Received Data Available flag by pulsing the Data Ready Reset input (pulser No. 1) each time that you wish to transmit and receive a new data word in this portion of the experiment, since we are not concerned with the Received Data Available flag.

This has been a complicated and somewhat long experiment for your first exposure to the UART chip, so a brief review of what you have done and observed may be helpful.

There is a definite relationship between the flags (Received Data Available, End of Character, and Transmitter Buffer Empty). Whenever an 8-bit data word is to be transmitted, the Data Strobe pin is pulsed. This loads the 8-bit data word into the transmitter buffer register. The Transmitter Buffer Empty flag goes to a logic zero to indicate that the buffer register is full and that no more data can be loaded into the UART. If the transmitter register is empty, the data in the transmitter buffer register are transferred to the transmitter register and the TBMT flag goes back to the logic one state to indicate that another data word may be entered into the UART.

The End of Character flag indicates that the transmitter has completed its transmission of all bits, start bits, data bits, parity bits (if any) and the stop bit(s).

The Received Data Available flag goes to a logic one to indicate that the transmitter has received the data bits and that they are available at the receiver outputs. The RDA flag does not wait for the stop bits, but goes to the logic one state when the data bits have been received. If you wish to use the RDA flag to indicate the receipt of a new data word, the flag must be reset by pulsing the Data Ready Reset input after the data word just received has been "used."

EXPERIMENT NO. 2

Purpose

The purpose of this experiment is to examine in detail the behavior of the UART Received Data Available (RDA), Transmitter Buffer Empty (TBMT), End of Character (EOC), and Serial Output (SO) signals. The circuit used in this experiment is the same as the one used in Experiment No. 1. This circuit will be used in Experiment No. 3, as well.

Schematic Diagram of Circuit

The schematic diagram of the circuit used in this experiment is the same as that used in Experiment No. 1. We refer you to Fig. 39 for the diagram, if you have not just performed Experiment No. 1.

Step 1

Replace the timing capacitor in your clock circuit with a 0.22- or 0.50-microfarad capacitor. This will slow the clock frequency to about 1.5 to 3 Hz. This is slow enough to allow you to observe the serial output at the SO pin, pin 25, as well as the operation of the various signal outputs, RDA, TBMT, and EOC.

Step 2

Examine the set of digital waveforms shown in Fig. 4-10.

You should note the following relationships between the input and output signals:

- A negative pulse applied to the Data Ready Reset input causes the Received Data Available flag output to go to a logic zero. This output will remain in the logic zero state until just after the final data bit of the 8-bit data word has been received and presented at the eight parallel receiver outputs.

A negative pulse applied to the Data Strobe input causes the End of Character, the Transmitter Buffer Empty and the Serial Output to all go to the logic zero state. The Transmitter Buffer Empty flag goes back to the logic one state very quickly.

Step 3

You should be familiar with the functions of the Data Strobe, Data Ready Reset, End of Character, Transmitter Buffer Empty, Received Data Available, and Serial Output signals. Briefly describe the functions of each, as it relates to the digital waveform presented in Fig. 40. Use the numbered arrows as a guide in making your notes in the following spaces provided.

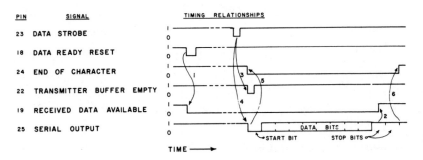

Fig. 40. Timing relationships for some UART control signals.

Data Strobe

Data Ready Reset

End of Character

Transmitter Buffer Empty

Received Data Available

Serial Output

A negative pulse applied to the Data Ready Reset input (pin 18) causes the Received Data Available output (pin 19) to go to a logic zero (1). The Received Data Available output will remain in the logic zero state until a complete 8-bit data word has been received (2). This occurs when all eight bits of data have been received by the receiver and are ready in parallel form.

A negative pulse applied to the Data Strobe input (pin 23) causes the End of Character (EOC), the Transmitter Buffer Empty (TMBT), and the Serial Output (SO) all to go to logic zero. The Transmitter Buffer Empty flag transition (3) indicates that the transmitter buffer is full, but only momentarily, since this flag goes back to a logic one state as soon as the data word has been transferred from the transmitter buffer to the transmitter register for transmission. The Serial Output goes to a logic zero (4), since a stop bit is being transmitted to indicate the start of a new data transmission. This in turn causes the End of Character flag output to go to a logic zero, since the transmitter is now in the transmit mode (5).

The Serial Output represents the stream of bits, including the data bits and the control bits.

The Received Data Available flag indicates that the 8-bit data word has been received and that it is available at the eight parallel outputs from the receiver section of the UART.

Step 4

Once the circuit shown in Fig. 39 has been wired, apply power to the circuit and reset the UART. Set the logic switches to 01010101. Remember that switch "H" is the most significant bit (MSB) and switch "A" is the least significant bit (LSB). Be sure that the clock signal has a frequency of no greater than 3 Hz. Actuate Pulser No. 1. This is the Data Ready Reset pulser. The lamp monitor connected to the Received Data Available flag output (pin 19) should be unlit, indicating that the Received Data Available flip-flop has been reset. This lamp monitor will not change if it was already unlit when this pulser was actuated.

Step 5

Prepare to press and release Pulser No. 2. This is the Data Strobe pulser. When you actuate this pulser, you will want to observe the status of the End of Character, Transmitter Buffer Empty, and Serial Output lamp monitors. Now, actuate the Data Strobe pulser and watch these three lamp monitors. Note your observations in the following space. You will have to wait for a minute or two, until the entire transmission has been completed. Remember that you are using a very slow clock and that 16 clock pulses are required for each transmission of a single bit.

We found that the Transmitter Buffer Empty flag went to a logic zero only for a short time, the period required for the transfer from the transmitter buffer register to the transmitter register.

The Received Data Available flag output went to a logic one state simultaneous with the availability of the new 8-bit data word at the eight parallel outputs of the receiver. This flag indicates that the eight parallel outputs now contain the data word just received.

The End of Character flag was still in the logic zero state when the complete set of eight data bits had been received. The End of Character flag indicates that all of the bits have been transmitted, not just the eight data bits. It remained in the logic zero state until the parity bit (if any) and the stop bit(s) have been transmitted.

You should be able to observe the serialized data bits, plus the start bit and stop bits at the Serial Output pin, SO, pin 25.

Step 6

Actuate Pulser No. 1, the Data Ready Reset pulser. You should observe that the Received Data Available output goes to a logic zero as this pulser is actuated. Why?

The Data Ready Reset input clears the Received Data Available flag so that it may be used again to detect the availability of the next data word.

You may wish to again transmit a data word to observe the states of these outputs. If you choose to do this, change the eight data bits to a new pattern. This will help you determine when the new pattern is available at the eight outputs of the receiver. Several transmissions may be required before you clearly see the relationship between these signals.

Step 7

Which of the UART flags could be used to indicate to an instrument that a new 8-bit data word has been received and is available at the eight parallel receiver outputs of the UART?

The Received Data Available flag could be used to indicate this.

What would the instrument have to do to the UART before it could detect the presence of the next 8-bit data word to be received?

The Received Data Available flag would have to be reset by pulsing the Data Ready Reset input.

Why would you not use the End of Character flag?

The EOC flag is associated with the transmitter, not the receiver!

EXPERIMENT NO. 3

Purpose

The purpose of this experiment is to demonstrate how you can count the number of bits that are transmitted by the UART. The operation of the parity bit is also explored.

Pin Configuration of Integrated Circuit (Fig. 41)

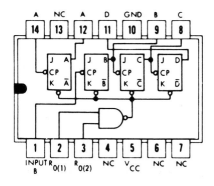

**Fig. 41. Pin configuration for SN7493 four-bit counter;
+5 volts to pin 5 and ground to pin 10.**

Schematic Diagram of Circuit (Fig. 42)

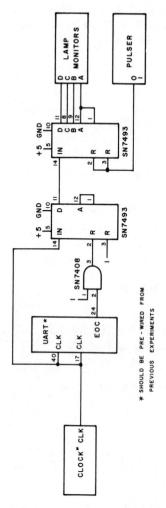

Fig. 42. Additional counter circuit required in Experiment No. 3 for UART bit counting.

Step 1

The basic UART circuit that was used in Experiment Nos. 1 and 2 will also be used in this experiment. We refer you to Fig. 39 in Experiment No. 1, if you do not have this circuit already wired.

An additional circuit must be wired to the UART. This is shown in Fig. 42. You may require an additional solderless breadboard to contain this additional circuitry.

Can you describe what the additional circuitry will do? Write a brief description of the circuit operation in the following space.

Two 4-bit binary counters have been added to the circuit. The SN7493 that has been connected directly to the CLOCK signal is a divide-by-16 counter that is enabled or turned on only when the UART transmitter is in the process of transmitting a stream of serial bits. Since the UART uses a clock that has a frequency that is 16 times the bit rate, the output of the first SN7493 counter will be a frequency that is equal to the actual bit rate.

The second SN7493 counter will count these pulses, one per bit and display the total number on the lamp monitors (or seven-segment display). Each of the bits, start bits, data bits, parity bit (if any) and stop bit(s) are counted in this way. This allows the total number of bits in the transmitted bit stream to be counted. At a slow enough clock frequency, you will be able to see the count being accumulated.

Step 2

Make the modifications shown in the schematic diagram in Fig. 42. We added the circuitry, but we used an additional breadboard so that the basic UART circuit would be relatively undisturbed.

After the circuit has been wired and power applied to it, adjust the clock so that it has a relatively slow frequency. We used a 0.1-microfarad capacitor with our clock for a frequency of approximately 7 Hz.

Step 3

Be certain that the −12-volt power supply has been connected to the UART and that the UART has been reset.

Set the logic switches at the transmitter inputs to 01010101. If you are using the LR-21 UART Outboard module, you will make changes to the logic levels at the programming pins or through the programming pins at the dual-in-line socket. If you are using the UART chip alone, you will make the changes at the UART pins, themselves. The programming pins are pins 35 through 39. Be certain that you can readily locate these pins.

Step 4

While the programming or control pins will be changed in various combinations during this experiment, the Control Strobe input, pin 34, *must remain at a logic one.*

Actuate the pulser that has been connected to the SN7493 counter. This will reset the counter so that the display should read zero. Be certain that the counter is always reset before you do any counting, otherwise an incorrect count will be accumulated.

Now, actuate the pulser that is connected to the UART Data Strobe input, Pulser No. 2. This will initiate the transmission of a data word. Since you are not concerned with the receiver section of the UART, it is not necessary to reset the Received Data Available flag. Thus, the pulser that is connected to the Data Ready Reset input does not have to be actuated.

Do you observe any changes at the lamp monitors? What was the final count that you observed?

We found that the lamp monitors slowly incremented a count from zero to 1011, or decimal 11. This indicated that 11 bits had been transmitted (one start bit, eight data bits, and two stop bits). Your observed count may have been different, since your UART control or programming pins may have been set in some other combination. If you did not observe any counting, carefully check your circuit. Remember to reset the UART whenever you apply power to it.

Change the UART control inputs, pins 35-39, so that they are all at a logic one state. Do not forget to reset the SN7493 counter. When you transmit a data word now, your count should total 11.

You do not have to be concerned with the eight bits of data that you are transmitting at this time.

Are you actually counting the bits as they are being transmitted?

No. You are only gating a counter so that it will count *at the same rate at which the bits are being transmitted*. The gating is provided by the transmitter End of Character (EOC) flag.

Step 5

Connect the No Parity control input, pin 35, to ground or logic zero. What will this do to the serial-bit stream?

It will place a parity bit in the serial stream of bits, just after the most significant bit (MSB) of data has been transmitted.

Now, transmit the data from the UART and count the number of bits that have been transmitted. You should be able to do this without further assistance. What count do you observe on the lamp monitors? Why?

We observed a count of 1100 or decimal 12. A start bit, eight data bits, a parity bit and two stop bits were transmitted, 12 bits in all.

Step 6

Connect pins 37 and 38 to logic zero. Now transmit the data word and count the number of bits that have been transmitted. What is the final count that you observe? What are the functions of the UART input pins, pins 37 and 38?

We observed that nine data bits were counted. The inputs at pins 37 and 38 control the number of bits in the data portion of the transmission.

Were your observations consistent with the use of pins 37 and 38?

Ours were. We observed nine bits, one start bit, five data bits, one parity bit and two stop bits. Remember, you added the parity bit in Step 5.

Step 7

What would be the shortest serial transmission that the UART could make? How would it be programmed at pins 35-39?

Once you have developed your answer, set the control pins accordingly and confirm your answer. We think that you should be familiar with the control inputs, so we will only say that a seven-bit transmission is the shortest that can be made by the UART. You should be able to figure out what those seven bits would represent.

Step 8

In the remaining portion of this experiment, you will examine the function of the parity bit and how it may be related to the set of data bits that are being transmitted by the UART.

If you do not have a lamp monitor connected to the UART Serial Output, pin 25, add one at this time. We refer you to Fig. 39 for a complete schematic of the UART circuit. Be sure to include the SN7408 buffer. The lamp monitor on the Serial Output will allow you to monitor the state of the bits that are being transmitted.

Be certain that the control bits are set as follow:

Pin 39 Parity Select   Logic 1
Pin 38 Number of Bits-1   Logic 0
Pin 37 Number of Bits-2   Logic 1
Pin 36 Stop Bits   Logic 1
Pin 35 No Parity   Logic 0

Pin 34 should be at a logic 1.

The serial stream of bits that would be sent when the transmitter is in this mode is shown in Fig. 43. Note that only seven bits of data are sent and that a parity bit has been placed in the serial bit stream. This represents a typical seven-bit transmission, with parity. Many computers and instruments use this type of data format.

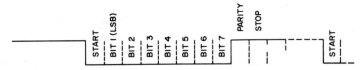

Fig. 43. Serial bit stream transmitted by UART in Experiment No. 3.

When the Parity Select control pin, pin 39, is a logic one and parity has been enabled (pin 35 at a logic zero), a logic one or a logic zero may be inserted in the parity bit position to give the data *even parity*. Recall that the definition of parity is:

Parity—A method of checking the accuracy or "correctness" of binary numbers. An extra *parity bit* is attached to binary numbers to do this. If even parity is used, the sum of the number of ones in the data word will be even. If odd parity is used, the sum of the number of ones will be odd. The parity bit is always included in the sum.

You are probably asking yourself, "Does the UART parity bit really work?" and, "Are the stop bits included in the parity determination, since they are always logic ones?"

Step 9

You will be able to observe the state of the parity bit on the lamp monitor that has been connected to the UART Serial Output pin. How will it be possible to determine which of the bits is really the parity bit?

The counter circuit will be used, since it increments its count each time that a bit has been transmitted. Thus, the start bit is observed while the counter output is zero, or 0000, the LSB of the data is observed when the count is 1, or 0001, and so on. The parity bit would be the one observed while the count is 1000, or eight. Again, do not forget to reset the counter before you attempt to count the bits.

The logic switches that are connected to the eight inputs of the transmitter should all be set to zero. Transmit the data word and observe the state of the lamp monitor connected to the Serial Output pin when the count is 1000, or eight. Note your observation:

Was the UART programmed for even or odd parity? Was it observed?

The UART should have been programmed for even parity (see Step 8). We found that the parity bit was a zero when the count was 1000.

Change the UART Stop Bits control input, pin 36, so that it is a logic zero. This will mean that only one stop bit will be transmitted, rather than two.

Reset the counter and again observe the state of the parity bit when the data are again transmitted.

What does this indicate about the relationship between the parity bit and the stop bits?

There is no relationship. The parity bit is not affected by the number of stop bits. When even parity was selected, the number of stop bits did not affect it. This would seem reasonable, since the stop bits are transmitted after the parity bit.

Return the Stop Bits control input, pin 36, to the logic one state.

Step 10

In this step, you will be provided with a number of 7-bit data words that are to be transmitted by the UART. A column labeled, "desired Parity" will indicate the parity that you should program into the UART through the use of the Parity Select input, pin 39, prior to the transmission of the data. In each case, you should attempt to predict the state of the parity bit before you actually try to observe it. We have provided a few answers that you may use as a guide:

Switch Settings G F E D C B A	Desired Parity	Parity Bit State Predicted	Observed
0 0 0 0 0 0 0	Even	0	0
0 0 0 0 0 0 0	Odd	1	1
0 0 0 0 0 0 1	Odd		
1 0 0 0 1 1 0	Even		
0 1 1 0 0 1 1	Even		
0 1 1 1 0 0 1	Odd		
0 1 1 0 1 0 1	Even		
1 1 1 1 1 1 1	Even		
1 1 1 1 1 1 1	Odd		

EXPERIMENT NO. 4

Purpose

The purpose of this experiment is to demonstrate the transmission of asynchronous-serial data between two UART integrated circuits in the full-duplex mode.

Schematic Diagram of Circuit (Fig. 44)

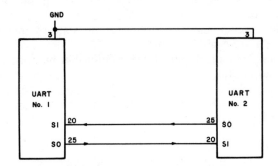

Fig. 44. Circuit changes necessary for two independent UARTs to communicate with each other.

Step 1

Two UART circuits will be required in this experiment. If you are performing these experiments with a friend, or in a class, we suggest that you attempt to transmit and receive the data from two separate UART chips. If you are working alone, you may use two UART chips on two separate breadboards.

Step 2

The UART circuit that you wired in Experiment No. 1 or No. 2 will also be used in this experiment. It is important that one of the

UARTs be selected and noted as UART No. 1 and the other as UART No. 2. This will allow us to readily distinguish between them in the text portion of the experiment.

If you have just completed Experiment No. 3, you may remove the two SN7493 counters and the lamp monitors associated with them, from your breadboard. Remember to keep the clock signal connected to your UARTs.

With the power to the UARTs disconnected or turned off, make the connections noted in the schematic diagram in Fig. 44. Also be certain that you remove the connection that was previously made between the output of the SN7408 buffer and the UART Serial Input pin, pin 20. Likewise, the lamp monitor or buffer connections to pins 19, 22, 24, and 25 should be removed.

Be certain that there is a good common ground connection between the two UART chips that you are using. This is very important, particularly if you are using two independent sets of power supplies. Two power supplies are *not* required, but their use further illustrates the transfer of data between two independent UART integrated circuits.

Step 3

Even though the two UART clock frequencies may not be within 3% of each other, try to transmit serial data between the two UART chips. Re-apply power to both of the UART circuits and attempt to transfer data from one to the other. Remember, this is done by actuating the pulser that has been connected to each UART Data Strobe input, pin 23. Be certain that both of the UARTs have been set to transmit and receive data in the same format. Vary the switch settings at each transmitter and attempt to transmit the data to the other UART. What, if anything, do you observe?

In our experiment, we found that the data bits were transferred from one UART to the other unreliably, if at all. This seemed to us to be an indication that the clock frequencies were outside of tolerance, i.e., they were not within 3% of each other.

We reduced the clock frequency of UART No. 1 by adding a 0.005-microfarad capacitor to the 0.05-microfarad capacitor that was already present at the clock. We used additional solderless terminals on our breadboard to make this parallel connection. This brought our two UART clocks to within the required 3% of each other. We were then able to transmit and receive the data reliably.

We concluded that *careful setting of the clocks was necessary before data could be transferred reliably between the two UART chips.*

Step 4

In this step, you will adjust the clock frequencies so that they are within 3% of each other. A smaller difference between the frequencies is better, if you can obtain it.

A frequency meter or period meter will be helpful in adjusting the two clocks. An oscilloscope is also useful. If, after several attempts to adjust the clock frequencies, you find that it is not possible with the components available, you may wish to use one of the clocks to control both of the UART circuits. This is acceptable in this experiment. In general, two crystal-based clocks or two readily adjustable clocks would eliminate this problem or that of trying to match the two frequencies.

Remember that a common clock would not be found in a true full-duplex transmission scheme.

Step 5

Once the two clocks have been set to be within 3% of each other, or a common clock has been wired into the circuits, transmit data from UART No. 1 to UART No. 2. Change the switch settings at UART No. 1 and confirm that they are being transmitted and received by UART No. 2. It is not necessary to reset the Received Data Available flag in this experiment.

Now, attempt to transmit eight data bits from UART No. 2 to UART No. 1. Again, change the switch settings and confirm that the data bits at the receiver section of UART No. 1 reflect these changes.

If you are not able to transmit data back and forth between the two UARTs, check for the common ground between the two UART circuits, check that the programming pins are properly set so that both UARTs have the same data format and, finally, check the clocks to be sure that they are still within 3% of each other.

Step 6

To confirm that data may be transferred in the full-duplex mode, the mode in which data are transferred in both directions at the same time, actuate both of the Data Strobe pulsers at the same time. This will cause data to be transmitted from UART No. 1 to UART No. 2 and from UART No. 2 to UART No. 1 at the same time. You may wish to change the switch settings to confirm that the data bits are actually changing.

If you are performing the experiment alone, the same pulser may be used to strobe both of the UARTs at the same time. A set of two lamp monitors may be used to observe the transmission of the data. Connect a lamp monitor to the Serial Output pin on each UART chip. You may wish to slow down the clock frequency so that this is easily observed.

The full duplex transmission mode is the most useful, but there are other transmission modes that we will also describe in some of the following experiments. These are:

Full-duplex—Information may be transferred in two directions at the same time. For example, the transfer of data from one UART to another at the same time that it is receiving data. Telephone transmissions are full-duplex, since information (speech) may be going in both directions at the same time. In teletypewriter circuits, a full-duplex scheme generally means one loop for the transmitter and another separate loop for the receiver.

Half-duplex—Information may be transferred in both directions, but in only one direction at a time. For example, radio transmissions, where one person transmits and then switches to the receive mode. One channel is shared by both the transmitter and receiver. Some teletypewriters operate in this mode.

Simplex—Information flows in one direction, from a transmitter to a receiver. Only one loop is used. Remote data acquisition systems that only transmit data to a data gathering system or a computer fit in this category.

EXPERIMENT NO. 5

Purpose

The purpose of this experiment is to explore the behavior of the error detection outputs, Parity Error (PE), pin 13 and Overrun (OR), pin 15. The basic UART circuit that was used in Experiment No. 4 will also be used in this experiment. Two independent UARTs are required in this experiment.

Schematic Diagram of Circuit (Fig. 45)

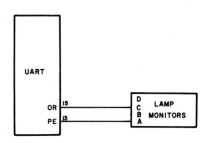

Fig. 45. Additions required to UARTs for Experiment No. 5 (Parity and Overrun Error flags may be monitored in this way).

The basic circuit that was used in Experiment No. 4 will also be used in this experiment. Two lamp monitors must be added to the circuit so that the logic state of two of the error detection flag outputs may be monitored. These lamp monitors should be added to both of the UARTs used in the circuit.

Step 1

With the power to both of the UARTs disconnected or turned off, make the *additions* to the two UART circuits, as shown in Fig. 45. The lamp monitors should be added to both of the UARTs. If only one set of lamp monitors is available, they should be added to the circuit for UART No. 2. If you choose to use this mode of operation, ignore all of the data transmission steps in which data are transmitted to UART No. 1.

Step 2

Set each UART No Parity pin, pin 35, to a logic zero (ground). This will program each UART to include the parity bit in its transmission and to check the parity of each data word received.

Step 3

Set the parity of UART No. 2 to "odd" and set the parity of UART No. 1 to "even." You should be able to do this without further assistance.

This step deliberately sets the UART chips so that their parity does not match.

Step 4

Set the data switches at both UART chips to logic ones. Now re-apply power to the UART circuits and reset both UART chips. Now, transmit data from UART No. 1 to UART No. 2. What is the state of the UART Parity Error output, pin 13, after the data has been received?

Transmit data from UART No. 2 to No. 1. What is the state of UART No. 1 Parity Error output, pin 13, after the data have been received?

We observed that the Parity Error output on each receiver went to a logic one after each data word had been received. This indicated that the parity of the data word was not what was expected. Is this what you should expect?

Yes, the parity settings on the UARTs were such that one was set for even parity and the other was set for odd parity.

Set the parity of UART No. 2 to "even" and repeat Step 4. Return here when you have done this.

What do you now observe at the Parity Error output at each UART?

We observed that the Parity Error outputs were logic zero when we did this. We would expect this, since the parity setting on both of the UARTs is now the same. Did you remember to reset your UART circuits?

Step 5

You may leave the parity control inputs as they are now set. In this step you will examine the operation of the Overrun Error output, pin 15.

In this step, UART No. 1 will be used as the transmitter and UART No. 2 will be used as the receiver. Preset the data word 10101010 on the data inputs to UART No. 1.

Actuate the Reset Data Available pulser that is connected to UART No. 2. Both of the lamp monitors, indicating Parity Error and Overrun Error, should be unlit or logic zero.

Actuate the Data Strobe pulser that is connected to UART No. 1. This will transmit the data to UART No. 2. Do either of the error outputs change state?

No. They should not. The parity setting at both UARTs is the same and there is no Overrun Error.

Again actuate the Data Strobe pulser connected to UART No. 1. After the transmission has been completed what are the states of the error outputs?

The Parity Error flag remains at a logic zero, while the Overrun Error output has become a logic one. Do you know why?

The Data Ready Reset pin on the UART (UART No. 2) has not been pulsed. This pulse would indicate to the receiving UART that the data that had been previously received was used. If it has not been pulsed, the UART indicates that the old data has been written over by the latest reception by indicating the Overrun Error condition.

Pulse the Data Ready Reset pulser at UART No. 2. The Overrun Error flag will now be tested again.

After you have reset the Received Data Available flag by pulsing the Data Ready Reset pin, pin 18 on the UART, retransmit the data word from UART No. 1 to UART No. 2. Does the Overrun Error flag on UART No. 2 change its state?

It should be a logic zero, since the Received Data Available flag was reset prior to this latest transmission. The Received Data Available flag should be a logic one, indicating that a new data word is present.

Reset the Received Data Available flag by actuating the Data Ready Reset pulser at UART No. 2. Now, again transmit the data from UART No. 1 to UART No. 2. What do you observe?

We observed that there was no Overrun Error and that the Received Data Available flag became a logic one when the data were received.

What would happen if the data word was again transmitted from UART No. 1 to UART No. 2? Try this. What do you observe? Is this what you would have predicted?

We found that the Received Data Available flag stayed at a logic one and the Overrun Error flag became a logic one. This is what we would expect.

EXPERIMENT NO. 6

Purpose

The purpose of this experiment is to interface a UART circuit with a 20-milliampere current loop that will be used to control a teletypewriter. The UART clock frequency will be adjusted to match that of the teletypewriter.

Schematic Diagram of Circuit (Fig. 46)

The schematic diagram of the simplex teletypewriter circuit is shown in Fig. 46. The basic UART circuit diagram has been presented in Experiment No. 1, Fig. 39. We refer you to it for the necessary circuit details. Note that pins 20 and 25 on the UART will no longer be connected to the SN7408 buffer and it may be removed from the circuit. The UART Serial Output and Serial Input pins will be connected to a current loop converter so that the UART will

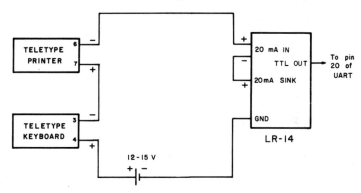

Fig. 46. Simplex current loop in which LR-14 Outboard module or equivalent circuitry is used (12- to 15-volt source used in current loop).

be able to communicate with a teletypewriter. The voltage source shown in Fig. 46 must be an isolated power supply with a voltage of between 12 and 15 volts. Two 6-volt lantern batteries are suggested.

A cathode-ray–tube terminal (CRT) may also be used in this and following experiments, if it has the capability to be interfaced to 20-mA current loops.

Step 1

Wire the circuit shown in Fig. 46. If you do not have an LR-14 Outboard module, the circuit shown in Fig. 31 may be wired instead. You should configure the UART so that it is set to receive a 7-bit word, without parity, but for two stop bits. The numbers shown in the "Teletype Printer" and "Teletype Keyboard" blocks in Fig. 46 represent the terminal block connections that are made to the teletypewriter terminal block.

Step 2

Most teletypewriters such as the Teletype Corporation ASR-33 model will operate at 10 characters per second, or 110 bits per second. This may also be noted as 110 baud. Since each bit will require 16 clock pulses, a UART clock frequency of 1760 Hz is required. You must adjust your clock so that it is within 3 to 5% of this.

Our clock circuit required that we use a capacitance of 440 picofarads, or two 220-picofarad capacitors in parallel to obtain the correct frequency. Small-value capacitors may be added to adjust the final frequency in your circuit so that the 1760 Hz signal is generated.

A digital frequency meter or an oscilloscope will prove to be very useful to obtain the correct frequency.

Step 3

Apply power to your system. Remember that power must be applied to both the UART system and to the current loop. The tele-typewriter must also be turned on by placing its control switch in the "LINE" position. If the UART clock is set so that it is within 3% of the required 1760 Hz, a character will be printed, and its code displayed at the UART receiver outputs, whenever a character key is depressed on the teletypewriter keyboard. The output observed at the receiver outputs may be either the binary code or the octal code of the character, depending on whether lamp monitors or seven-segment displays have been used.

If the teletypewriter "chatters," the wiring of the 20-mA current loop is incorrect. Some of the common problems that we have observed are:

- The +5-volt power is not connected to the UART or to the LR-14 TTL/20-mA Current Loop Outboard module. Check the equivalent circuit if you are not using the LR-14 Outboard module.
- The ground connections at the UART or at the current converter circuit are not correct.
- The teletypewriter current loop leads have been reversed.

If these suggestions are not helpful, we suggest that you ask an instructor or obtain further assistance before going on.

Step 4

Once the teletypewriter and the UART have been connected properly, the teletypewriter printer mechanism should not "chatter" when the system has power applied to it.

With power applied to the system, actuate the "0" key (zero). Observe the output of the UART receiver. You should see 060_8 or 0110000_2. If you observed a 260 or 10110000_2, you may wish to disconnect the connection between the UART receiver MSB and the display. Now, ground the MSB of the display. In this way, only the least significant seven bits of data are displayed.

If you depress the "A" key, you should observe that the UART output is 101_8 or 1000001_2.

If you did not observe these outputs, and if you did not observe the printing of the equivalent character on the printer mechanism, the UART clock is probably not adjusted so that it is within 3% of the required 1760-Hz clock frequency. You will have to stop at this point and adjust the clock frequency until the UART receives the data reliably from the teletypewriter keyboard. You may use the "0" and "A" keys to check your adjustment.

Once you have made the proper adjustments, consult the ASCII code chart in the appendix and correlate several other keys to their corresponding codes.

After several keys have been successfully tested, go on to the next experiment.

EXPERIMENT NO. 7

Purpose

The purpose of this experiment is to show how characters may be transmitted from the keyboard on the teletypewriter and received by the UART. The codes of the characters will be displayed in either the binary or octal code, depending on the kind of display that has been connected to the UART receiver section.

Schematic Diagram of Circuit

The circuit that will be used in this experiment is the same one that was used in Experiment No. 6. We refer you to Figs. 39 and 46 for the circuit details. If you are starting the experiments here, we recommend that you go back to Experiment No. 6 for the details of adjusting your UART clock. If you have just completed Experiment No. 6, no changes to the circuit are required.

Step 1

Apply power to your system (Teletypewriter, UART, and 20-mA current loop). In turn, actuate the teletypewriter keyboard keys listed in the following chart. Note the octal or binary values in the columns provided:

In this experiment you should observe that there is a correspondence between the values output by the receiver section of the UART and the ASCII character codes presented in the text. If this is not the case, we suggest that you check the clock frequency that you are using.

Many teletypewriters and terminals, even though they use the ASCII code, are incompatible. Why is this? Would you expect this?

Key	Binary Data	Octal Data
0	0110000	060
1		
4		
9		
A		
C		
G		
K		
O		
S		
U		
Z		
&		
%		
!		
.		

There are many possible combinations of stop bits, parity bits; even parity, odd parity, and possibly, no parity. Even the data words may be seven or eight bits long. This is expected, but it usually does not present too many difficulties, since the UART control pins may be

Key	Binary Data	Octal Data
0		
1		
4		
9		
A		
C		
G		
K		
O		
S		
U		
Z		
&		
%		
!		
.		

switched between logic one and logic zero to program it to be compatible with the particular terminal in question.

As a continuation of this experiment, program your UART so that it is set to transmit and receive eight bits of data.

Step 2

Retransmit the characters that were noted in STEP 1, and note the 8-bit octal or binary code for each one in the chart below:
What does the most significant bit represent?

Depending on the teletypewriter used, this bit may be a logic zero, a logic one, or it may reflect the parity of the data.

EXPERIMENT NO. 8

Purpose

The purpose of this experiment is to examine the operation of the transmitter section of the UART. Some ASCII-based character codes will be transmitted from the UART to the teletypewriter.

Schematic Diagram of Circuit (Fig. 47)

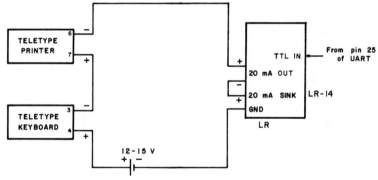

Fig. 47. Current loop connections for Experiment No. 7 (UART used to transmit data to teletypewriter—12- to 15-volt source used in current loop).

The schematic diagram of the current loop circuit that will be used in this experiment is shown in Fig. 47. Note that the only changes that have to be made are to remove the connection to the UART receiver and to connect the UART transmitter to the LR-14 current converter Outboard module (or equivalent circuit) and to change the connection of the current loop to the converter Outboard module.

Step 1

Make the connection between the UART transmitter output (Serial Output, pin 25) and the TTL IN pin on the LR-14 Outboard module. Be sure that the connection between the TTL OUT signal on the LR-14 Outboard module and the UART Serial In pin, pin 20, has been removed. Move the current loop connections to the 20-mA OUT pins, as shown in Fig. 47. The power to the system should be disconnected while you make these changes. The basic UART circuit is still used.

Step 2

Depress several of the teletypewriter keys and examine the lamp monitors or seven-segment displays that are connected to the UART receiver outputs. Do you observe any changes as the keys are actuated?

You should not. The connection between the UART receiver and the current loop has been disconnected.

Step 3

Connect the UART programming pins so that it will send seven data bits, a parity bit, and two stop bits. The state of the parity bit may be either even or odd. You should be able to do this without further assistance.

Step 4

Apply power to your system. Set the seven least significant bit logic switches as shown in the following table. Once a setting has been made, transmit the data to the teletypewriter by actuating the Data Strobe pulser that is connected to pin 23 on the UART. You should observe the printing of recognizable characters on the tele-typewriter. You may have to switch to the opposite parity of the setting now used, to obtain the desired characters. This is a function of the kind of teletypewriter that you are using and what it has been set to receive.

Logic Switch Settings	Character Printed
0 1 1 0 0 0 0	0 (zero)
0 1 1 0 0 1 1	
1 0 0 0 0 0 1	
0 1 0 0 0 0 0	
1 0 1 0 1 0 0	
1 0 0 0 1 0 1	
1 0 1 0 0 1 1	
1 0 1 0 1 0 0	

How can you determine that the results that you have obtained are the correct ones?

You can match the results that you obtained with the ones that you would expect, by using an ASCII code chart, such as the one in the appendix. Hint, you should see a message.

EXPERIMENT NO. 9

Purpose

The purpose of this experiment is to demonstrate the use of the half-duplex mode of the UART-teletypewriter system. In a half-duplex system, data may be transmitted in either direction, UART to teletypewriter or teletypewriter to UART, but not simultaneously.

Schematic Diagram of Circuit (Fig. 48)

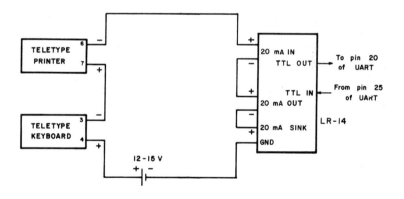

Fig. 48. Current loop connections for half-duplex operation of teletypewriter-UART circuit (12- to 15-volt source used in current loop).

Step 1

The circuit that you have used in Experiments Nos. 7 and 8 is used in this experiment. If you have completed Experiment No. 8, you will need to make the connection between the LR-14 Outboard module TTL OUT pin and the Serial Input pin, pin 20, on the UART. The current loop connections must also be changed, as noted in Fig. 48.

Step 2

You will find that this experiment is a combination of Experiments Nos. 7 and 8. In those experiments, you transmitted data from the teletypewriter to the UART and then you transmitted data from the UART to the teletypewriter. This was a *simplex* scheme, since data was transferred in only one direction.

In the half-duplex transmission scheme, data may be transmitted and received by either the UART or teletypewriter, but it cannot be done by both simultaneously.

Apply power to your system. The teletypewriter must be in the "LINE" mode and current must be present in the loop. The teletype should not "chatter" in this mode if the power is correctly applied and the circuit is working.

Step 3

In the half-duplex mode, you should be able to depress the keys on the teletypewriter keyboard and have the ASCII character codes displayed on the lamp monitors or seven-segment displays that are connected to the UART receiver data outputs.

Depress the keys noted in the following chart and note your observations in the space provided. The UART should be programmed for eight data bits, no parity, and two stop bits.

Key	Binary Data	Octal Data
0		
1		
4		
9		
A		
C		
G		

Do your results compare with those obtained in Experiment No. 7? Are the results consistent with the data in the ASCII chart?

With the teletypewriter that we used, the results were consistent. Remember that in Experiment No. 7, the UART was set to receive a 7-bit data word, rather than the 8-bit data word that we have now programmed it for. Your results may be different, if your teletypewriter uses the most significant bit (MSB) of the data word as a parity bit, or if it is always preset to a logic one or a logic zero. The seven least significant bits should match the ASCII chart information.

Step 4

You may wish to transmit additional codes to the UART from the keyboard. If you do, you should observe that the codes in the ASCII chart match the codes that have been transmitted.

Step 5

In this step, the UART will be used to transmit characters to the teletypewriter printer. This is similar to the operation that was performed in Experiment No. 8.

Transmit each of the 8-bit data words noted in the following chart to the printer. Remember that the Data Strobe pulser must be actuated to transmit each 8-bit word. Note the resultant action in the space provided in the chart:

Step 7

It should be fairly obvious that you cannot transmit from the UART and the teletypewriter at the same time. Why?

Logic Switch Settings	Observed Operation
0 0 0 0 1 1 0 1	
0 0 0 0 1 0 1 0	
0 1 0 0 0 0 0 1	
0 0 1 0 0 0 0 0	
0 1 0 0 1 1 1 1	
0 1 0 0 1 0 1 1	
0 0 0 0 0 1 1 1	

Are your observations consistent with what is expected?

They should be. If you are in doubt, find the equivalent ASCII character code in the ASCII chart.

Step 6

You may wish to transmit other characters to the teletypewriter. You should observe that these are consistent with the information presented in the ASCII chart.

Two of the devices are trying to break the current loop at the same time. The data transmission will be badly "garbled."

Let us now prove that this is so. With whatever data is present at the UART data inputs, transmit the character to the teletypewriter. If this is a nonprinting character, choose another one that will print a character, for example, 01000001 or "A." Now transmit this character to the teletypewriter.

Depress a key on the keyboard. Does the ASCII character code appear on the seven-segment display?

We found that an "A" was printed and the code for a question mark was available at the UART outputs from the receiver section.

Now, attempt to transmit the character from the UART and from the keyboard simultaneously. This means that the key must be actuated at the same time that the UART Data Strobe input is pulsed.

What do you observe at the UART data outputs and on the paper of the printer? You may wish to repeat this several times.

We observed data values and characters that bore no resemblance to what was supposed to have been transmitted by either the UART or the teletypewriter.

If your transmissions do not overlap, then the data from the keyboard and the UART will be received properly.

Step 8

One thing that you should note in this experiment is that since all of the receiving devices are in the same loop, any code transmitted by the keyboard or by the UART will be received by *both* the teletypewriter printer and by the UART receiver section.

To confirm this, depress several of the keyboard keys and note the action at both the printer and at the displays that are connected to the UART receiver outputs.

There are many instances when this type of loop is used, for example in control applications where new control information or commands are sent to all of the "stations" on the loop. In many cases, each station will have its own identifier code so that internal circuitry will only accept commands that are intended for that particular station.

EXPERIMENT NO. 10

Purpose

The purpose of this experiment is to use the UART-teletype-writer circuit in the full-duplex mode. Data will be transferred between the teletypewriter and the UART simultaneously.

Schematic Diagram of Circuit (Fig. 49)

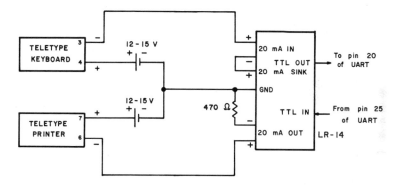

Fig. 49. Circuit for full-duplex data transfers between teletypewriter and UART (one or two 12- to 15-volt sources used in loop and 470-ohm resistor used to limit current—see text).

Step 1

The circuit that will be used in this experiment is quite similar to the one used in Experiments Nos. 6 through 9. Note that only the connections in the current loop need to be changed if you have just completed Experiment No. 9. If the connections to both the UART receiver and transmitter have not been made, be sure to connect them, as noted in Fig. 49.

Two independent current loops are required for this experiment. Although two independent power supplies are shown in Fig. 49, one power supply may be used. To use a single supply, simply remove one and connect the positive terminals on the "Teletype Printer" (7) and on the "Teletype Keyboard" (4) together. The remainder of the circuit remains the same. If a single power supply is used it must, of course, be capable of providing 40 milliamperes of current.

Wire the circuit shown in Fig. 49.

Step 2

One of the current loops uses the 20-mA current sink circuit that is provided on the LR-14 Outboard module or in the equivalent circuitry. Another current sink is needed and a 470-ohm resistor has been used to provide this current limiting.

Apply power to the system. Remember to connect all of the power supplies. The teletypewriter switch should be in the "LINE" position. The teletype should not "chatter" if it is connected to the loop properly.

Step 3

Depress several of the keys on the teletypewriter keyboard. Does the printer print them? It should not, since it has not been wired into the keyboard current loop. As you type various characters (keys) the corresponding codes should appear as the equivalent ASCII codes on the UART receiver outputs.

As you actuate additional keys, the correspondence between the keys and the ASCII codes should be apparent. You should not require additional help to make this correspondence.

Step 4

Preset the eight data inputs to the UART transmitter so that the 8-bit data word 00110000 will be transmitted. Remember, the UART should be programmed to transmit an 8-bit data word, no parity, and two stop bits.

Transmit the character to the teletypewriter. Is it received and printed?

We observed that a "0" was printed. If you need a clean line, either transmit a 00001101 and a 00001010, or switch the teletypewriter to the "LOCAL" mode and actuate the Return and Line keys. Place the teletypewriter in the "LINE" mode.

Transmit some other 8-bit codes that have "printing" equivalents. Do any of these codes appear at the UART receiver outputs?

No. The UART-to-teletypewriter loop has been isolated from the UART receiver section.

Step 5

With the UART transmitter inputs set to transmit one of the printing characters, attempt to transmit simultaneously a character from the keyboard to the UART receiver section. Can this be done? How? What do you observe when you try this?

Yes, it can be done, since the two loops are independent of each other. To do it, simply actuate the Data Strobe pulser on the transmitter section of the UART at the same time that you actuate a key on the teletypewriter keyboard. You should observe that the printing character code is printed and that the keyboard code is available at the receiver outputs.

In a full-duplex system, such as this, simultaneous data transfers are allowed. This is the kind of system that is generally used to connect teletypewriters and terminals with computers.

ASCII Code Chart

LEAST SIGNIFICANT BITS

	000	001	010	011	100	101	110	111	
00000	NUL	SOH	STX	ETX	EOT	ENQ	ACK	BEL	CONTROL
00001	BS	HT	LF	VT	FF	CR	SO	SI	FUNC-
00010	DLE	DCl	DC2	DC3	DC4	NAK	SYN	ETB	TIONS
00011	CAN	EM	SUB	ESC	FS	GS	RS	US	
00100	SP	!	"	#	$	%	&	"	
00101	(	)	*	+	,	—	.	/	
00110	0	1	2	3	4	5	6	7	
00111	8	9	:	;	<	=	>	?	
01000	@	A	B	C	D	E	F	G	
01001	H	I	J	K	L	M	N	O	
01010	P	Q	R	S	T	U	V	W	
01011	X	Y	Z	[	\	]	↑	—	
01100	'	a	b	c	d	e	f	g	
01101	h	i	j	k	l	m	n	o	
01110	p	q	r	s	t	u	v	w	
01111	x	y	z	{	:	}	∿	DEL	

MOST SIGNIFICANT BITS

Control Character Functions

NUL	= Null	DLE	= Data Link Escape
SOH	= Start of Heading	DC1	= Device Control 1
STX	= Start of Text	DC2	= Device Control 2
ETX	= End of Text	DC3	= Device Control 3
EOT	= End of Transmission	DC4	= Device Control 4 (Stop)
ENQ	= Enquiry	NAK	= Negative Acknowledge
ACK	= Acknowledge	SYN	= Synchronous Idle
BEL	= Bell (ring)	ETB	= End of Transmission Block
BS	= Backspace	CAN	= Cancel
HT	= Horizontal Tabulation	EM	= End of Medium
LF	= Line Feed	SUB	= Substitute
VT	= Vertical Tabulation	ESC	= Escape
FF	= Form Feed	FS	= File Separator
CR	= Carriage Return	GS	= Group Separator
SO	= Shift Out	RS	= Record Separator
SI	= Shift In	US	= Unit Separator
		DEL	= Delete

Data Rate and
Clock Frequency Table

Data Rate (b/sec)	Clock Rate (Hz)		
	1 X	16 X*	64 X
50	50	800	3200
110	110	1760	7040
150	150	2400	9600
300	300	4800	19.2 K
600	600	9600	38.4 K
1200	1200	19.2 K	76.8 K
2400	2400	38.4 K	153.6 K
4800	4800	76.8 K	307.2 K
9600	9600	153.6 K	614.4 K

* Unless otherwise noted, most UARTs require a clock frequency that is sixteen times the data rate, in bits per second (b/sec)

List of USART and UART Manufacturers

Advanced Micro Devices
901 Thompson Place
Sunnyvale, CA 95086

American Microsystems, Inc.
3800 Homestead Road
Santa Clara, CA 95051

Exar Integrated Systems, Inc.
750 Palomar Avenue
Sunnyvale, CA 94088

Fairchild Semiconductor
464 Ellis Street
Mountain View, CA 94042

General Instruments Corp.
600 West John Street
Hicksville, NY 11802

Harris Semiconductor
P. O. Box 883
Melbourne, FL 32901

Intel Corp.
3065 Bowers Avenue
Santa Clara, CA 95051

Intersil, Inc.
10900 N. Tantau Avenue
Cupertino, CA 95014

Motorola Semiconductor
  Products, Inc.
P. O. Box 20912
Phoenix, AZ 85036

National Semiconductor Corp.
2900 Semiconductor Drive
Santa Clara, CA 95051

NEC Microcomputers, Inc.
5 Militia Drive
Lexington, MA 02173

Signetics Corp.
811 East Arques Avenue
Sunnyvale, CA 94086

Texas Instruments Incorporated
P. O. Box 5012
Dallas, TX 75222

Western Digital Corp.
3128 Red Hill Avenue
Newport Beach, CA 92663

Zilog, Inc.
10460 Bubb Road
Cupertino, CA 95014

APPENDIX D

Data Sheet for
TMS 6011 UART IC

A data sheet for the Texas Instruments TMS 6011, a general UART integrated circuit. *Courtesy of Texas Instruments Incorporated, Dallas, TX.*

These data sheets have been provided for general informational use only. Complete up-to-date data sheets should be obtained directly from the manufacturer for additional information and complete electrical specifications. Inclusion of this technical information does not necessarily imply endorsement by either the authors or the publisher.

- Transmits, receives, formats data
- Full-duplex or half-duplex operation
- Operation from dc to 200 kHz
- Static logic
- Buffered parallel inputs and outputs
- Programmable word lengths — 5, 6, 7, 8 bits
- Programmable information rate
- Programmable parity generation/verification
- Programmable parity inhibit
- Automatic data formatting
- Automatic status generation
- 3-state push-pull buffers
- Low-threshold technology
- Standard power supplies: +5 V, −12 V
- Full TTL compatibility — no external components
- Dual-in-line package — ceramic or plastic

description

The TMS 6011 JC, NC is an MOS/LSI subsystem designed to ensure the data interface between a serial communicator link and data processing equipment such as a peripheral or computer. The device is referred to in the industry as an asynchronous data interface or as Universal Asynchronous Receiver/Transmitter (UART).

The receiver section of the TMS 6011 will accept serial data from the transmission line and convert it to parallel data. The serial word will have start, data, and stop bits. Parity may be generated and verified. The receiver section will validate the received data transmission by checking proper start, parity, and stop bits, and convert the data to parallel.

The transmitter section will accept parallel data, convert it to serial form and generate the start, parity, and stop bits.

Receiver and transmitter sections are separate and the device can operate in full duplex mode.

The TMS 6011 is a fully programmable circuit allowing maximum flexibility of operation, defined as follows:

- The device can operate either in full-duplex (simultaneous transmission and reception) or in half-duplex mode (alternate transmission and reception).

- The data word may be externally selected to be 5, 6, 7, or 8 bits long.

- Baud rate is externally selected by the clock frequency. Clock frequency can vary between 0 and 200 kHz.

- Parity, which is generated in the transmit mode and verified in the receive mode, can be selected as either odd or even. It is also possible to disable the parity bit by inhibiting the parity generation and verification.

- The stop bit can be selected as either a single- or a double-bit stop.

- Static logic is used to maximize flexibility of operation and to simplify the task of the user. The data holding registers are static and will hold a data word until it is replaced by another word.

— continued

TMS 6011 JC, NC
ASYNCHRONOUS DATA INTERFACE (UART)

description (continued)

To allow for a wide range of possible configurations, 3-state push-pull buffers have been used on all outputs except serial-transmitter and **TREmpty** flag. They allow the wire-OR configuration.

The TMS 6011 can be used in a wide range of data handling equipment such as Modems, peripherals, printers, data displays, and minicomputers. By taking full advantage of the latest MOS/LSI design and processing techniques it has been possible to implement the entire transmit, receive, and format function necessary for digital data communication in a single package, avoiding the cumbersome circuitry previously necessary.

P-channel enhancement-mode low-threshold technology permits the use of standard power supplies (+5 V, −12 V) as well as direct TTL/DTL interface. No external components are needed.

The device is available in both a 40-pin dual-in-line ceramic package (TMS 6011 JC) and a 40-pin plastic package (TMS 6011 NC).

operation

The operation can be best understood by visualizing the TMS 6011 as three separate sections: 1) transmitter, 2) receiver, and 3) common control. The transmitter and receiver sections are independent while the control section directs both receive and transmit.

transmitter section

The transmitter section will accept data in parallel form, serialize it, format it, and transmit it in serial form.

Parallel input data is received on the transmitter-buffer-register data inputs TR_1 through TR_8.

Serial output data is transmitted on the **TROutput** terminal.

Input data is stored in the transmitter-buffer register. A logic Low on the **TBRLoad** command terminal will load a character in the transmitter-buffer register. If words of less than 8 bits are used, only the least significant bits are accepted. The character is justified into the least significant bit, TR_1.

The data is transferred to the transmitter register when **TBRLoad** terminal goes from Low to High. The loading of the transmitter register is delayed if the transmitter section is presently transmitting data. In this case the loading of the transmitter register is delayed until the transmission has been performed.

Output serial data (transmitted on the **TROutput** terminal) is clocked out by **TRClock**. The clock rate is 16 times faster than the data rate.

The data is formatted as follows: start bit, data, parity bit, stop bits (1 or 2). Start bits, parity bits, and stop bits are generated by the TMS 6011. When no data is transmitted the output **TROutput** sits at a logic High.

The start of transmission is defined as the transition of **TROutput** from a logic High to a logic Low.

Two flags are provided. A logic High on the **TBREmpty** flag indicates that a word has been transferred to the transmitter/receiver and that the transmitter buffer receiver is now ready to accept a new word. A logic High on the **TREmpty** flag indicates that the transmitter section has completed the transmission of a complete word including stop bits. The **TREmpty** flag will sit at a logic High until the start of transmission of a new word.

Both transmitter holding register and transmitter registers are static and will perform dc storage of data.

functional block diagram

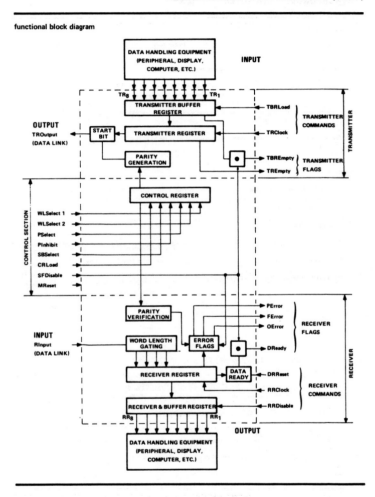

operation (continued)

receiver section

The data is received in serial form on the receive input RInput.

The data is presented in parallel form on the eight data outputs RR_1 through RR_8.

RInput is the data input terminal. The data from RInput enters the receiver register at a point determined by the character length, the parity, and the number of stop bits. RInput must be maintained High when no data is being received. The data is clocked through the RR clock. The clock rate is 16 times faster than the data rate.

Data is transferred from the receiver register to the receiver buffer register and appears on the 8 RR outputs. The MOS output buffers used for the eight RR terminals are 3-state push-pull output buffers which permit the wire-OR configuration through use of the RRDisable terminal. When a logic High is applied to RRDisable, the RR outputs are floating. If the word length is less than 8 bits, the most significant bits will be at a logic low. The output word is right justified. RR_1 is the least significant bit and RR_8 is the most significant bit.

A logic low applied to the DRReset terminal resets the DReady output to a logic Low.

Several flags are provided in the receiver section. There are three error flags (parity error, framing error and overrun error) and a data-ready flag. All status flags may be disabled through a logic High on the SFDisable terminal.

A logic High on the PError terminal indicates an error in parity.

A logic High on the FError terminal indicates a framing error that is an invalid or nonexistent stop bit in the received word.

A logic High on the OError terminal indicates an overrun. An overrun occurs when the previous word has not been read, i.e., when the DReady line has not been reset before the present data was transferred to the data-receive holding register.

A logic High on the DReady terminal indicates that a word has been received, stored in the receiver-buffer register and that the data is available on outputs RR_1 through RR_8. The DReady terminal can be reset through the DRReset terminal.

common control section

The common control section will direct both the receiver and the transmitter sections.

The initialization of the TMS 6011 is performed through the MReset terminal. The Master Reset is strobed to a logic High after power turn-on to reset all registers and to reset the serial output line to a logic High.

All status flags (parity error, framing error, overrun error, data ready, transmitter buffer register) are disabled when the SFDisable is at a logic High. When disabled, the status flags float (3-state buffers in high-impedance state).

The number of bits per word is controlled by the WLSelect 1 and WLSelect 2 lines. The word length may be 5, 6, 7, or 8 bits. The selection is as follows:

WORD LENGTH	WLS_1	WLS_2
5	Low	Low
6	High	Low
7	Low	High
8	High	High

operation (concluded)

common control section (continued)

The parity to be checked by the receiver and generated by the transmitter is determined by the **PSelect** line. A logic High on the **PSelect** line selects even parity and a logic Low selects odd parity.

The parity will not be checked or generated if a logic High is applied to **PInhibit**; in this case the stop bit or bits will immediately follow the data bit.

When a logic High is applied to **PInhibit**, the **PError** status flag is brought to a logic Low, indicating a no-parity error because parity is disregarded in this mode.

To select either one or two stop bits, the **SBSelect** terminal is used. A logic High on this terminal will result in two stop bits while a logic Low will produce only one.

To load the control bits (**WLSelect 1, WLSelect 2, PSelect, PInhibit, SBSelect**) a logic High is applied to the **CRLoad** terminal. This terminal may be strobed or hardwired to a logic High.

absolute maximum ratings over operating free-air temperature range (unless otherwise noted)

Supply voltage V_{DD} range (See Note 1) . . . . −20 V to 0.3 V
Supply voltage V_{GG} range (See Note 1) . . . . −20 V to 0.3 V
Clock input voltage range (See Note 1) . . . . −20 V to 0.3 V
Data input voltage range (See Note 1) . . . . −20 V to 0.3 V
Operating free-air temperature range . . . . −25°C to 85°C
Storage temperature range . . . . −55°C to 150°C

NOTE 1: These voltage values are with respect to V_{SS} (substrate).

recommended operating conditions

PARAMETER	MIN	NOM	MAX	UNIT
Operating Voltage				
Substrate supply, V_{SS}	+4.75	5.0	5.25	V
Drain supply, V_{DD}		0		V
Gate supply, V_{GG}	−12.5	−12	−11.5	V
Logic Levels (See Note 2)				
Input High level, V_{IH}	V_{SS} −1.5		V_{SS} +0.3	V
Input Low level, V_{IL}	−12		0.8	V
Clock Voltage Levels (See Note 2)				
Clock High level, $V_{\phi H}$	V_{SS} −1.5		V_{SS} +0.3	V
Clock Low level, $V_{\phi L}$	−12		0.8	V
Clock Frequency (See Note 3)	dc		200	kHz

NOTES: 2. All data, clock, and command inputs have internal pull-up resistors to allow direct clock by any TTL logic circuit.

3. Clock frequency is 16 times baud rate.

— continued

recommended operating conditions (continued)

PARAMETER	MIN	NOM	MAX	UNIT
Pulse Width				
Clock Pulse	2.5			μs
Transmitter Buffer Register Load TBRL	400			ns
Control Strobe CRL	250			ns
Parity Inhibit PI (See Note 4)	400			ns
Parity Select PS (See Note 4)	300			ns
Word Length Select WLS1, WLS2, Stop Bit Select SBS (See Note 4)	200			ns
Master Reset	1.5			μs
Data Ready Reset DRR	250			ns
Input Data and Control (See Timing Diagram – transmitter)				
Set-up time	10			ns
Hold time	20			ns

NOTE 4: PI, PS, WLS$_1$, WLS$_2$ and SBS are normally static signals. A minimum pulse width has been indicated for possible pulsed operation.

static electrical characteristics, nominal operating conditions, $T_A = -25°C$ to $85°C$ (unless otherwise noted)

	PARAMETER	TEST CONDITIONS	MIN	TYP*	MAX	UNIT
I_{IH}	Input Current Logic High	$V_{IN} = 5\,V$			10	μA
$I_{\phi H}$	Clock Current Logic High	$V_{IN} = 5\,V$			10	μA
I_{IL}	Input Current Logic Low	$V_{IN} = 0\,V$			1.6	mA
$I_{\phi L}$	Clock Current Logic Low	$V_{IN} = 0\,V$			1.6	mA
Output Voltage Levels						
V_{OL}	Output Low Level	$I = 1.6\,mA$			0.6	V
V_{OH}	Output High Level	$I = 200\,μA$	2.4			V
Power Supply Current Drain		All inputs Logic High				
I_{SS}	Substrate supply			20	30	mA
I_{GG}	Gate supply			7	12	mA
P_D	Power dissipation			190	300	mW

dynamic electrical characteristics, nominal operating conditions, $T_A = -25°C$ to $85°C$ (unless otherwise noted)

	PARAMETER	TEST CONDITIONS	MIN	TYP*	MAX	UNIT
Output Logic Delay (See timing diagram – receiver)						
t_{DL}	Output Low level	One TTL load		300	500	ns
t_{DH}	Output High level	One TTL load		300	500	ns
Reset Delay (DRR to DR)				0.8	1	μs
Flag Output Delay (SFD to Flag)		SFD_{LH}			500	ns
		SFD_{HL}			300	ns
Capacitance						
C_{IN}	All inputs	$V_{IN} = V_{SS}, \ f = 1\,MHz$		10	20	pF
C_ϕ	Clock	$V_{IN} = V_{SS}, \ f = 1\,MHz$		10	20	pF

* Typical values are at 25°C.

timing diagram and voltage waveforms

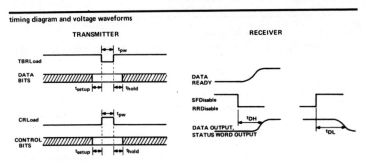

mechanical data and pin assignment

The device is available in both a 40-pin hermetically sealed ceramic dual-in-line package (TMS 6011 JC) and a 40-pin plastic package (TMS 6011 NC). These packages are designed for insertion in mounting-hole rows on 0.600-inch centers.

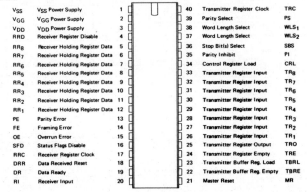

V_SS	V_SS Power Supply	1		40	Transmitter Register Clock	TRC
V_GG	V_GG Power Supply	2		39	Parity Select	PS
V_DD	V_DD Power Supply	3		38	Word Length Select	WLS_1
RRD	Receiver Register Disable	4		37	Word Length Select	WLS_2
RR_8	Receiver Holding Register Data	5		36	Stop Bit(s) Select	SBS
RR_7	Receiver Holding Register Data	6		35	Parity Inhibit	PI
RR_6	Receiver Holding Register Data	7		34	Control Register Load	CRL
RR_5	Receiver Holding Register Data	8		33	Transmitter Register Input	TR_8
RR_4	Receiver Holding Register Data	9		32	Transmitter Register Input	TR_7
RR_3	Receiver Holding Register Data	10		31	Transmitter Register Input	TR_6
RR_2	Receiver Holding Register Data	11		30	Transmitter Register Input	TR_5
RR_1	Receiver Holding Register Data	12		29	Transmitter Register Input	TR_4
PE	Parity Error	13		28	Transmitter Register Input	TR_3
FE	Framing Error	14		27	Transmitter Register Input	TR_2
OE	Overrun Error	15		26	Transmitter Register Input	TR_1
SFD	Status Flags Disable	16		25	Transmitter Register Output	TRO
RRC	Receiver Register Clock	17		24	Transmitter Register Empty	TRE
DRR	Data Received Reset	18		23	Transmitter Buffer Reg. Load	TBRL
DR	Data Ready	19		22	Transmitter Buffer Reg. Empty	TBRE
RI	Receiver Input	20		21	Master Reset	MR

TTL interface circuit

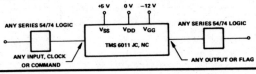

TMS 6011 JC, NC
ASYNCHRONOUS DATA INTERFACE (UART)

operation timing diagram

TRANSMITTER TIMING[†]

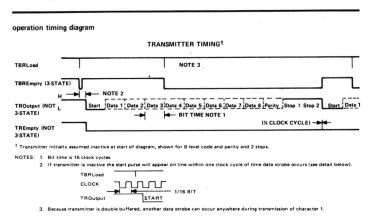

[†] Transmitter initially assumed inactive at start of diagram, shown for 8 level code and parity and 2 stops.

NOTES: 1. Bit time is 16 clock cycles.
2. If transmitter is inactive the start pulse will appear on line within one clock cycle of time data strobe occurs (see detail below).

3. Because transmitter is double buffered, another data strobe can occur anywhere during transmission of character 1.

RECEIVER TIMING

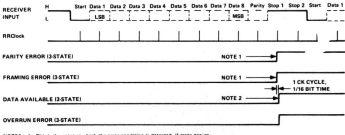

NOTES: 1. This is the point at which the error condition is detected, if error occurs.
2. Data available is set only when the received data has been transferred to the buffer register. Data available going High also transfers PE, FE, or the status word holding register (see block diagram).
3. All information is good in buffer register until data available tries to set for next character.
4. Above shown for 8-level code, parity and 2-stop. For no parity, stop bits follow data.
5. For all-level code, the data in the buffer register must be right-justified, i.e., RD$_1$ (pin 12).

Data Sheet for TR 1863A/B-Type UART IC

A data sheet for the Western Digital TR1863A/B-type UART, a single-supply–type UART integrated circuit. *Courtesy of Western Digital Corporation, Newport Beach, CA.*

These data sheets have been provided for general informational use only. Complete up-to-date data sheets should be obtained directly from the manufacturer for additional information and complete electrical specifications. Inclusion of this technical information does not necessarily imply endorsement by either the authors or the publisher.

MOS/LSI

TR1863A/B

ASYNCHRONOUS RECEIVER/TRANSMITTER

FEATURES

- SILICON GATE TECHNOLOGY — LOW THRESHOLD circuitry
  Directly TTL and CMOS Compatible
- SINGLE POWER SUPPLY — +5 VDC ONLY
- D.C. STABLE (STATIC) CIRCUITRY
- FULL DUPLEX OR HALF DUPLEX OPERATION
  Transmits and Receives Serial Data Simultaneously or Alternately
- AUTOMATIC INTERNAL SYNCHRONIZATION OF DATA AND CLOCK
- AUTOMATIC START BIT GENERATION
- BUFFERED RECEIVER AND TRANSMITTER REGISTERS
- FULLY PROGRAMMABLE — EXTERNALLY SELECTABLE
  Word Length
  Baud Rate
  Even/Odd Parity (Reciver/Verification — Transmitter/Generation)
  Parity Inhibit — Verification/Generation
  One, One and One-Half, or Two Stop Bit Generation
- AUTOMATIC DATA RECEIVED/TRANSMITTED STATUS GENERATION
  Transmission Complete   Parity Error
  Buffer Register Transfer Complete   Framing Error
  Received Data Available   Overrun Error
- THREE-STATE OUTPUTS
  Receiver Register Outputs
  Status Flags
- AVAILABLE IN CERAMIC OR HERMETIC PLASTIC CAVITY PACKAGES

APPLICATIONS

PERIPHERALS	CARD AND TAPE READERS
TERMINALS	PRINTERS
MINI COMPUTERS	DATA SETS
FACSIMILE	CONTROLLERS
TRANSMISSION	KEYBOARD ENCODERS
MODEMS	REMOTE DATA
CONCENTRATORS	ACQUISITION SYSTEMS
ASYNCHRONOUS DATA	ASYNCHRONOUS DATA
MULTIPLEXERS	CASSETTES

PIN CONNECTIONS
*NOTE: NC means No Connection.

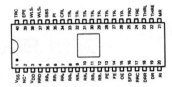

TR1863A CERAMIC PACKAGE

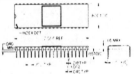

TR1863B PLASTIC PACKAGE

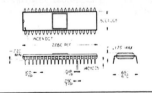

GENERAL DESCRIPTION

The TR1863A and the TR1863B are ASYNCHRONOUS RECEIVER/TRANSMITTER subsystems using silicon gate process technology. The use of this low threshold process provides direct compatibility with all forms of current sinking logic. Interfacing restraints, such as external resistors, drivers and level shifting circuitry, are eliminated. All output lines have been designed to drive TTL directly.

The ASYNCHRONOUS RECEIVER/TRANSMITTER is a general purpose, programmable MOS/LSI device for interfacing an asynchronous serial data channel of a peripheral or terminal with parallel data of a computer or terminal. The transmitter section converts parallel data into a serial word which contains the data along with start, parity, and stop bits. The receiver section converts a serial word with start, data, parity, and stop bits, into parallel data, and it verifies proper code transmission by checking parity and receipt of a valid stop bit. Both the receiver and the transmitter are double buffered. The array is compatible with bipolar logic. The array may be programmed as follows: The word length can be either 5, 6, 7, or 8 bits; parity generation and checking may be inhibited, the parity may be even or odd; and the number of stop bits may be either one or two, with one and one half when transmitting a 5 bit code. NOTE: See TR1402A Data Sheet for operation with 5 level code-2 stop bits.

TRANSMITTER FLOW CHART　　　　RECEIVER FLOW CHART

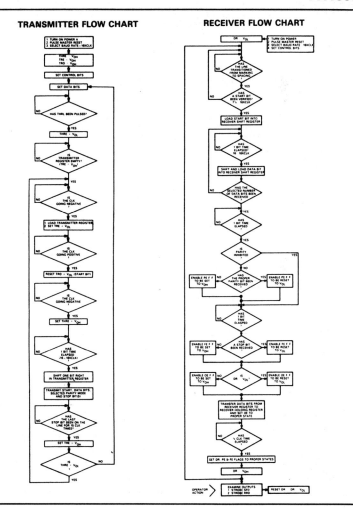

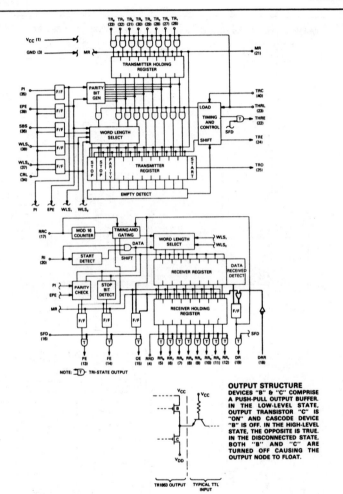

OUTPUT STRUCTURE
DEVICES "B" & "C" COMPRISE A PUSH-PULL OUTPUT BUFFER. IN THE LOW-LEVEL STATE, OUTPUT TRANSISTOR "C" IS "ON" AND CASCODE DEVICE "B" IS OFF. IN THE HIGH-LEVEL STATE, THE OPPOSITE IS TRUE. IN THE DISCONNECTED STATE, BOTH "B" AND "C" ARE TURNED OFF CAUSING THE OUTPUT NODE TO FLOAT.

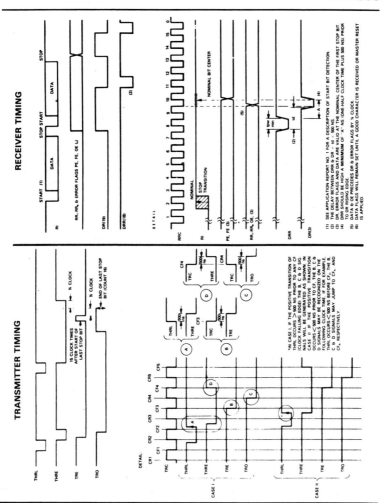

PIN DEFINITIONS

PIN NUMBER	NAME	SYMBOL	FUNCTION
1	V_{SS} POWER SUPPLY	V_{SS}	+ 5 volts supply
2		NC	No Connection (Open)
3	GROUND	GND	Ground = 0V
4	RECEIVER REGISTER DISCONNECT	RRD	A high level input voltage, V_{IH}, applied to this line disconnects the RECEIVER HOLDING REGISTER outputs from the RR_8 RR_1 data outputs (pins 5-12).
5-12	RECEIVER HOLDING REGISTER DATA	RR_8-RR_1	The parallel contents of the RECEIVER HOLDING REGISTER appear on these lines if a low-level input voltage, V_{IL}, is applied to RRD. For character formats of fewer than eight bits received characters are right-justified with RR_1 (pin 12) as the least significant bit and the truncated bits are forced to a low level output voltage, V_{OL}.
13	PARITY ERROR	PE	A high level output voltage, V_{OH}, on this line indicates that the received parity does not compare to that programmed by the EVEN PARITY ENABLE control line (pin 39). This output is updated each time a character is transferred to the RECEIVER HOLDING REGISTER. PE lines from a number of arrays can be bussed together since an output disconnect capability is provided by Status Flag Disconnect line (pin 16).
14	FRAMING ERROR	FE	A high-level output voltage, V_{OH}, on this line indicates that the received character has no valid stop bit, i.e., the bit (if programmed) is not a high level voltage. This output is updated each time a character is transferred to the Receiver Holding Register. FE lines from a number of arrays can be bussed together since an output disconnect capability is provided by Status Flag Disconnect line (pin 16).
15	OVERRUN ERROR	OE	A high-level output voltage, V_{OH}, on this line indicates that the Data Received Flag (pin 19) was not reset before the next character was transferred to the Receiver Holding Register. OE lines from a number of arrays can be bussed together since an output disconnect capability is provided by Status Flag Disconnect line (pin 16).
16	STATUS FLAGS DISCONNECT	SFD	A high-level input voltage, V_{IH}, applied to this pin disconnects the PE, FE, OE, DR and THRE allowing them to be buss connected.
17	RECEIVER REGISTER CLOCK	RRC	The receiver clock frequency is sixteen (16) times the desired receiver shift rate.
18	DATA RECEIVED RESET	DRR	A low-level input voltage, V_{IL}, applied to this line resets the DR line.
19	DATA RECEIVED	DR	A high-level output voltage, V_{OH}, indicates that an entire character has been received and transferred to the RECEIVER HOLDING REGISTER.
20	RECEIVER INPUT	RI	Serial input data received on this line enters the RECEIVER REGISTER at a point determined by the character length, parity, and the number of stop bits. A high-level input voltage, V_{IH}, must be present when data is not being received.
21	MASTER RESET	MR	This line is strobed to a high-level input voltage, V_{IH}, to clear the logic. It resets the Transmitter and Receiver Registers, the Receiver Holding Register, FE, OE, PE, DRR and sets TRO, THRE, and TRE to a high-level output voltage, V_{OH}.
22	TRANSMITTER HOLDING REGISTER EMPTY	THRE	A high-level output voltage, V_{OH}, on this line indicates the TRANSMITTER HOLDING REGISTER has transferred its contents to the TRANSMITTER REGISTER and may be loaded with a new character.
23	TRANSMITTER HOLDING REGISTER LOAD	THRL	A low-level input voltage, V_{IL}, applied to this line enters a character into the TRANSMITTER HOLDING REGISTER. A transition from a low-level input voltage, V_{IL}, to a high-level input voltage, V_{IH}, transfers the character into the TRANSMITTER REGISTER if it is not in the process of transmitting a character. If a character is being transmitted, the transfer is delayed until its transmission is completed. Upon completion, the new character is automatically transferred simultaneously with the initiation of the serial transmission of the new character.
24	TRANSMITTER REGISTER EMPTY	TRE	A high-level output voltage, V_{OH}, on this line indicates that the TRANSMITTER REGISTER has completed serial transmission of a full character including STOP bit(s). It remains at this level until the start of transmission of the next character.
25	TRANSMITTER REGISTER OUTPUT	TRO	The contents of the TRANSMITTER REGISTER (START bit, DATA bits, PARITY bit, and STOP bits) are serially shifted out on this line. When no data is being transmitted, this line will remain at a high-level output voltage, V_{OH}. Start of transmission is defined as the transition of the START bit from a high-level output voltage V_{OH} to a low-level output voltage, V_{OL}.

PIN DEFINITIONS (CONT)

PIN NUMBER	NAME	SYMBOL	FUNCTION
26-33	TRANSMITTER REGISTER DATA INPUTS	TR_1- TR_8	The character to be transmitted is loaded into the TRANSMITTER HOLDING REGISTER on these lines with the THRL Strobe. If a character of less than 8 bits has been selected (by WLS_1 and WLS_2), the character is right justified to the least significant bit, RR1, and the excess bits are disregarded. A high-level input voltage, V_{IH}, will cause a high-level output voltage, V_{OH}, to be transmitted.
34	CONTROL REGISTER LOAD	CRL	A high-level input voltage, V_{IH}, on this line loads the CONTROL REGISTER with the control bits (WLS_1, WLS_2, EPE, PI, SBS). This line may be strobed or hard wired to a high-level input voltage, V_{IH}.
35	PARITY INHIBIT	PI	A high-level input voltage, V_{IH}, on this line inhibits the parity generation and verification circuits and will clamp the PE output (pin 13) to V_{OL}. If parity is inhibited the STOP bit(s) will immediately follow the last data bit on transmission.
36	STOP BIT (S) SELECT	SBS	This line selects the number of STOP bits to be transmitted after the parity bit. A high-level input voltage, V_{IH}, on this line selects two STOP bits, and a low-level input voltage, V_{IL}, selects a single STOP bit. Selection of two STOP bits when programming a five (5) bit word generates 1.5 STOP bits.
37-38	WORD LENGTH SELECT	WLS_2 WLS_1	These two lines select the character length (exclusive of parity) as follows:
39	EVEN PARITY ENABLE	EPE	This line determines whether even or odd PARITY is to be generated by the transmitter and checked by the receiver. A high-level input voltage, V_{IH}, selects even PARITY and a low-level input voltage, V_{IL}, selects odd PARITY.
40	TRANSMITTER REGISTER CLOCK	TRC	The transmitter clock frequency is sixteen (16) times the desired transmitter shift rate.

WLS_2	WLS_1	Word Length
V_{IL}	V_{IL}	5 bits
V_{IL}	V_{IH}	6 bits
V_{IH}	V_{IL}	7 bits
V_{IH}	V_{IH}	8 bits

MAXIMUM RATINGS

C_{CC} Supply Voltage	$-0.3V$ to $+7.0V$
Clock Input Voltage*	$-0.3V$ to $+7.0V$
Logic Input Voltage*	$-0.3V$ to $+7.0V$
Logic Output Voltage*	$-0.3V$ to $+7.0V$
Storage Temperature	$-55°C$ to $+150°C$
Operating Free-Air Temperature T_A Range	$0°C$ to $+70°C**$
Lead Temperature (Soldering, 10 sec.)	$300°C$

*GND = OV
NOTE: These voltages are measured with respect to GND

ELECTRICAL CHARACTERISTICS

$V_S = V_{CC} = 5V \pm 5\%$, $V_{DD} = 0V$ $\qquad$ $T_A = 0°C$ to $+70°C$ unless otherwise specified

SYMBOL	PARAMETER	MIN.	MAX.	CONDITIONS
I_{CC}	OPERATING CURRENT Supply Current		35 ma	$V = 5.25V$
V_{IH}	LOGIC LEVELS Logic High	2.4V		
V_{IL}	Logic Low		0.6V	$V_{SS} = 4.75V$
V_{OH} .	OUTPUT LOGIC LEVELS Logic High	2.4V		$V_{SS} = 4.75V$, $I_{OH} = -100 \mu a$
V_{OL}	Logic Low		0.4V	$V_{SS} = 5.25V$, $I_{OL} = 1.6$ ma
I_{OS}*	Short Circuit Current		20ma	$V_{SS} = 5.25V$, $V_O = 0V$
I_{OC}	Output Leakage		10 a	$V_{OUT} = 0V$, SFD = RRD = V_{IH}
I_{IL}	Input Current		$+10ua$	$V_{IN} = V_{IH}$ or V_{IL}

*Only one output should be shorted at any time.
**Consult factory for extended temperature range UARTS.

SWITCHING CHARACTERISTICS —
See "Switching Waveforms"

$V_{CC} = 5V$, $V_{DD} = 0V$ $\qquad$ $T_A = 25°$, $C_{LOAD} = 20$ pf plus one TTL load

SYMBOL	PARAMETER	MIN.	MAX.	CONDITIONS
f_{clock}	Clock Frequency	D.C.	1.0 MHz*	$V_{SS} = 4.75V$
t_{pw}	Pulse Widths CRL THRL DRR MR	200 ns 200 ns 200 ns 500 ns		(See figures 1 & 2)
t_c	Coincidence Time	200 ns		(See figures 1 & 2)
t_{hold}	Hold Time	20 ns		(See figures 1 & 2)
t_{set}	Set Time	0		(See figure 1 & 2)
t_{pd0}	OUTPUT PROPAGATION DELAYS To Low State		250 ns	(See figure 3) $C_L = 20$ pf, plus one TTL load
t_{pd1}	To High State		250 ns	(See figure 3) $C_L = 20$ pf, plus one TTL load
c_{in}	CAPACITANCE Inputs		20 pf	$f = 1$ MHz, $V_{in} = 5V$
c_o	Outputs		20 pf	$f = 1$ MHz, $V_{in} = 5V$

*f_{max} for TR1863A or B = 1.0 MHz
f_{clock} may be factory selected for 3.5 MHz max.

SWITCHING WAVEFORMS

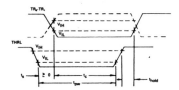

Figure 1. Data Input Load Cycle

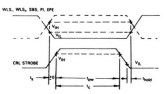

Figure 2. Control Register Load Cycle

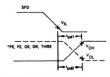

Figure 3. Status Flag Output Delays

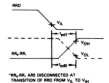

Figure 4. Data Output Delays

Data Sheet for IM6402 and IM6403 CMOS UART IC

A data sheet for the Intersil IM6402 and IM6403 CMOS UART integrated circuits. *Courtesy of Intersil, Inc., Cupertino, CA.*

These data sheets have been provided for general informational use only. Complete up-to-date data sheets should be obtained directly from the manufacturer for additional information and complete electrical specifications. Inclusion of this technical information does not necessarily imply endorsement by either the authors or the publisher.

FEATURES

- Operation from DC to 3.2 MHz
- Low Power - typ.<10mW @ 3.2MHz
- 4V-11V Operation
- Programmable Word Length, Stop Bits and Parity
- Automatic Data Formatting and Status Generation
- Compatible with Industry Standard UART's
- Crystal Operation—IM6403

CMOS/LSI UNIVERSAL ASYNCHRONOUS RECEIVER TRANSMITTER (UART) IM6402/6403 IM6402A/6403A

GENERAL DESCRIPTION

The IM6402 and IM6403 are CMOS/LSI subsystems for interfacing computers or microprocessors to an asynchronous serial data channel. The receiver converts serial start, data, parity and stop bits to parallel data verifying proper code transmission, parity, and stop bits. The transmitter converts parallel data into serial form and automatically adds start, parity, and stop bits. The data word length can be 5, 6, 7 or 8 bits. Parity may be odd or even. Parity checking and generation can be inhibited. The stop bits may be one or two or one and one-half when transmitting 5 bit code.

The IM6402 and IM6403 can be used in a wide range of applications including modems, printers, peripherals and remote data aquisition systems. CMOS/LSI technology permits operating clock frequencies up to 3.2 MHz (200K Baud) an improvement of 10 to 1 over previous PMOS UART designs. Power requirements, by comparison, are reduced from 300mw to 10mw. Status logic increases flexibility and simplifies the user interface.

The IM6402 differs from the IM6403 on pins 2, 17, 19, 22, and 40 as shown in the connection diagram. The IM6403 utilizes pin 2 as a control and pins 17 and 40 for an inexpensive crystal oscillator as shown on page 5. TBREmpty and DReady are always active. All other input and output functions of the IM6402 and IM6403 are as described.

ORDERING INFORMATION

CIRCUIT MARKING AND PRODUCT CODE EXPLANATION

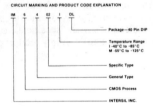

PACKAGE DIMENSIONS

DL 40 Pin DIP

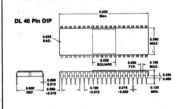

CONNECTION DIAGRAM

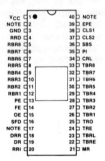

NOTE:	PIN	IM6402	IM6403
	2	N/C	CONTROL
	17	RRC	OSC IN
	40	TRC	OSC OUT

INTERSIL, INC., 10900 N. TANTAU AVE., CUPERTINO, CA 95014

Printed in U.S.A.

(408) 996-5000 TWX 910-338-0228

1 of 6

CMOS TO CMOS

IM6402A/03A

ABSOLUTE MAXIMUM RATINGS

Supply Voltage	+12.0V
Input or Output Voltage Applied	GND -.05V to VCC+0.5V
Storage Temperature Range	-65°C to 150°C
Operating Temperature Range	
Industrial IM6402A/03AI	-40°C to +85°C
Military IM6402A/03AM	-55°C to +125°C

DC CHARACTERISTICS V_{CC} = 4V to 11V, T_A = Industrial or Military

PARAMETER	SYMBOL	CONDITIONS	MIN	TYP	MAX	UNITS
Logical "1" Input Voltage	V_{IH}		70% VCC			V
Logical "0" Input Voltage	V_{IL}				20% VCC	V
Input Leakage	I_{IL}	OV VIN VCC	-1.0		1.0	µA
Logical "1" Output Voltage	V_{OH}	IOUT = 0	VCC - 0.01			V
Logical "0" Output Voltage	V_{OL}	IOUT = 0			GND + 0.01	V
Output Leakage	I_O	OV Vo VCC	-I.0		I.0	µA
Supply Current IM6402A/03A	I_{CC}	VIN = VCC		5.0	500	µA
Input Capacitance	C_{IN}			7.0	8.0	pF
Output Clearance	C_O			6.0	10.0	pF

AC CHARACTERISTICS V_{CC} = 10.0V, C_L = 50pF, T_A = 25°C

PARAMETER	SYMBOL	CONDITIONS	MIN	TYP	MAX	UNITS
Clock Frequency	f_{clock}		D.C		6.4	MHz
Pulse Widths CRL, DRR, TBRL	t_{pw}			100		ns
Pulse Width MR	t_{pw}	See switching time		250		ns
Input Data Setup Time	t_{SET}	waveforms 1, 2, 3		50		ns
Input Data Hold Time	t_{HOLD}			50		ns
Output Propagation Delays	t_{pd}			100		ns

SWITCHING WAVEFORMS

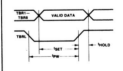

FIGURE 1.

DATA INPUT CYCLE

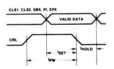

FIGURE 2.

CONTROL REGISTER LOAD CYCLE

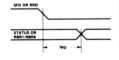

FIGURE 3.

STATUS FLAG OUTPUT DELAYS OR DATA OUTPUT DELAYS

CMOS TO TTL

ABSOLUTE MAXIMUM RATINGS

Supply Voltage	+7.0V
Input or Output Voltage Applied	GND −0.3V to V_{CC}+0.3V
Storage Temperature Range	−65°C to +150°C
Operating Temperature Range Industrial IM6402/03I	−40°C to +85°C
Military IM6402/03M	−55°C to +125°C

DC CHARACTERISTICS V_{CC} = 5.0 +− 10%. T_A = Operating Temperature Range

PARAMETER	SYMBOL	CONDITIONS	MIN	TYP	MAX	UNITS
Logical "1" Input Voltage	V_{IH}		V_{CC}-2.0			V
Logical "0" Input Voltage	V_{IL}				0.8	V
Input Leakage	I_{IL}	0V < V_{IN} < V_{CC}	−1.0		1.0	μA
Logical "1" Output Voltage	V_{OH2}	I_{OUT} = 0	V_{CC} -0.01			V
Logical "1" Output Voltage	V_{OH1}	I_{OH} = −0.2 mA	2.4			V
Logical "0" Output Voltage	V_{OL2}	I_{OUT} = 0			GND +0.01	V
Logical "0" Output Voltage	V_{OL1}	I_{OL} = 2.0 mA			0.45	V
Output Leakage	I_O	0V < V_O < V_{CC}	−1.0		1.0	μA
Supply Current	I_{CC}	V_{IN} = GND or V_{CC}: Output Open		1.0	100	μA
Input Capacitance	C_{IN}			7.0	8.0	
Output Capacitance	C_O			8.0	10.0	pF

AC CHARACTERISTICS V_{CC} = 5.0V, T_A = 25°C

PARAMETER	SYMBOL	CONDITIONS	MIN	TYP	MAX	UNITS
Clock Frequency	f_{clock}		D.C		3.2	MHz
Pulse Widths CRL, DRR, TBRL	t_{pw}			200		ns
Pulse Width MR	t_{pw}	See switching time		500		ns
Input Data Setup Time	t_{SET}	waveforms 1, 2, 3		100		ns
Input Data Hold Time	t_{HOLD}			100		ns
Output Propagation Delays	t_{pd}			200		ns

IM6403 UNIVERSAL ASYNCHRONOUS RECEIVER TRANSMITTER WITH ON CHIP 4/11 STAGE DIVIDER

The IM6403 differs from the IM6402 on three inputs, TRC, RRC, and pin 2, and two outputs TBRE and DR.

Outputs DR and TBRE are not three-state, but are always active.

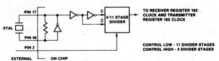

The divider chain output acts as a 16X clock to both the receiver register and transmitter register. Consequently both receiver and transmitter operate at the same frequency. The TRClock and RRClock inputs are used for a crystal oscillator while pin 2 controls the number of divider stages.

The on chip divider and oscillator allow an inexpensive crystal to be used as a timing source rather than additional circuitry such as baud rate generators. For example, a color TV crystal at 3.579545MHz results in a baud rate of 109.2 Hz for an easy teletype interface.

FUNCTIONAL BLOCK DIAGRAM

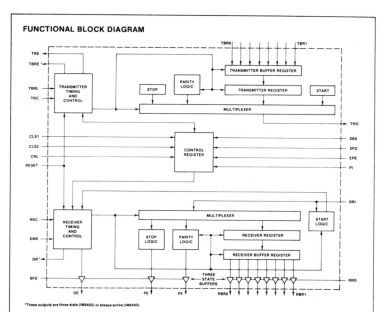

*These outputs are three state (IM6402) or always active (IM6403).

TRANSMITTER OPERATION

The transmitter section accepts parallel data, formats it and transmits it in serial form on the TROutput terminal. (A) Data is loaded into the transmitter buffer register from the inputs TR1 through TR8 by a logic low on the TBRLoad input. Valid data must be present at least t_{SET} prior to and t_{HOLD} following the rising edge of TBRL. If words less than 8 bits are used, only the least significant bits are used. The character is right justified into the least significant bit, TR1. (B) The rising edge

of TBRL clears TBREmpty. ½ to 1½ clock cycles later data is transferred to the transmitter register and TREmpty is cleared. ½ cycle later transmission starts. Output data is clocked by TRClock. The clock rate is 16 times the data rate. ½ clock cycle later TBREmpty is reset to a logic high. (C) A second pulse on TBRLoad loads data into the transmitter buffer register. Data transfer to the transmitter register is delayed until transmission of the current character is complete. (D) Data is automatically transferred to the transmitter register and transmission of that character begins one clock cycle later.

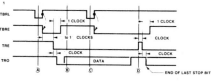

TRANSMITTER TIMING (NOT TO SCALE)

RECEIVER OPERATION

Data is received in serial form at the RInput. When no data is being received, RInput must remain high. The data is clocked through the RRClock. The clock rate is 16 times the data rate. (A) A low level on DRReset clears the DReady line. (B) During the first stop bit data is transferred from the receiver register to the RBRegister. If the word is less than 8 bits, the unused most significant bits will be a logic low. The output character is right justified to the least significant bit RBR1. A logic high on OERror indicates overruns. An overrun occurs when DReady has not been cleared before the present character was transferred to the RBRegister. (C) ½ clock cycle later DReady is reset to a logic high, PError and FError are evaluated. A logic high on FError indicates an invalid stop bit was received, a framing error. A logic high on PError indicates a parity error.

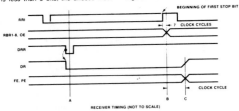

RECEIVER TIMING (NOT TO SCALE)

START BIT DETECTION

The receiver uses a 16X clock for timing. (A) the start bit could have occurred as much as one clock cycle before it was detected, as indicated by the shaded portion. The center of the start bit is defined as clock count 7½. If the receiver clock is a symetrical square wave, the center of the start bit will be located within ±½ clock cycle, ±¹⁄₃₂ bit or ±3.125% giving a receiver margin of 46.875%. The receiver begins searching for the next start bit at the center of the first stop bit.

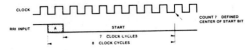

INTERFACING WITH THE IM6100 MICROPROCESSOR

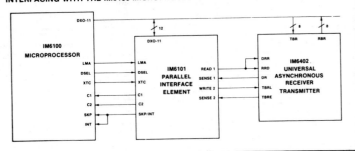

PIN ASSIGNMENT AND FUNCTIONS

PIN	SYMBOL	DESCRIPTION
1	VCC	+5 Volts Supply
2	IM6402-N/C IM6403-Control	No Connection 4/11 Stage Divider High: 4 Stage Low: 11 Stage
3	GND	Ground
4	RRD	A High level on RECEIVER REGISTER DISABLE forces the receiver holding register outputs RBR1-RBR8 to a high impedance state.
5	RBR8	The contents of the RECEIVER BUFFER REGISTER appear on these three-state outputs. Word formats less than 8 characters are right justified to RBR1.
6	RBR7	See Pin 5 - RBR8
7	RBR6	See Pin 5 - RBR8
8	RBR5	See Pin 5 - RBR8
9	RBR4	See Pin 5 - RBR8
10	RBR3	See Pin 5 - RBR8
11	RBR2	See Pin 5 - RBR8
12	RBR1	See Pin 5 - RBR8

PIN	SYMBOL	DESCRIPTION
13	PE	A high level on PARITY ERROR indicates received parity does not match parity programmed by control bits. When parity is inhibited this output is low.
14	FE	A high level on FRAMING ERROR indicates the first stop bit was invalid.
15	OE	A high level on OVERRUN ERROR indicates the data received flag was not cleared before the last character was transferred to the receiver buffer register.
16	SFD	A high level on STATUS FLAGS DISABLE forces the outputs PE, FE, OE, DR, TBRE to a high impedance state.
17	IM6402-RRC IM6403-OSCIN	The RECEIVER REGISTER CLOCK is 16X the receiver data rate.
18	DRR	A low level on DATA RECEIVED RESET clears the data received outputDR, to a low level.
19	DR	A high level on DATA RECEIVED indicates a character has been received and transferred to the receiver buffer register.
20	RRI	Serial data on RECEIVER REGISTER INPUT is clocked into the receiver register.

IM6402/03

PIN	SYMBOL	DESCRIPTION
21	MR	A high level on MASTER RESET clears PE, FE, OE, and DR to a low level and sets the transmitter output to a high level.
22	TBRE	A high level on TRANSMITTER BUFFER REGISTER EMPTY indicates the transmitter buffer register has transferred its data to the transmitter register and is ready for new data.
23	TBRL	A low level on TRANSMITTER BUFFER REGISTER LOAD transfers data from inputs TBR1-TBR8 into the transmitter buffer register. A low to high transition on TBRL indicates data transfer to the transmitter register. If the transmitter register is busy, transfer is automatically delayed so that the two characters are transmitted end to end.
24	TRE 6	A high level on TRANSMITTER REGISTER EMPTY indicates completed transmission of a character including stop bits.
25	TRO	Character data, start data and stop bits appear serially at the TRANSMITTER REGISTER OUTPUT.
26	TBR1-TBR8	Character data is loaded into the TRANSMITTER BUFFER REGISTER via inputs TBR1-TBR8. For character formats less than 8 bits the TBR8, 7, and 6 inputs are ignored corresponding to the programmed word length.

PIN	SYMBOL	DESCRIPTION
27	TBR2	See Pin 26 - TBR1
28	TBR3	See Pin 26 - TBR1
29	TBR4	See Pin 26 - TBR1
30	TBR5	See Pin 26 - TBR1
31	TBR6	See Pin 26 - TBR1
32	TBR7	See Pin 26 - TBR1
33	TBR8	See Pin 26 - TBR1
34	CRL	A high level on CONTROL REGISTER LOAD loads the control register.
35	PI	A high level on PARITY INHIBIT inhibits parity generation, parity checking and forces PE output low.
36	SBS	A high level on STOP BIT SELECT selects 1.5 stop bits for 5 character format and 2 stop bits for other lengths.
37	CLS2	These inputs program the CHARACTER LENGTH SELECTED. (CLS1 low CLS2 low 5 bits) (CLS1 high CLS2 low 6 bits) (CLS1 low CLS2 high 7 bits) (CLS1 high CLS2 high 8 bits)
38	CLS1	See Pin 37 - CLS2
39	EPE	When PI is low a high level on EVEN PARITY ENABLE generates and checks even parity. A low level selects odd parity
40	IM6402-TRC IM6403-OSCOUT	The TRANSMITTER REGISTER CLOCK is 16X the transmit data rate.

Data Sheet for
8251A USART IC

A data sheet (abridged) for the Intel 8251A USART integrated circuit. *Reprinted by permission of Intel Corporation, Santa Clara, CA.*

These data sheets have been provided for general informational use only. Complete up-to-date data sheets should be obtained directly from the manufacturer for additional information and complete electrical specifications. Inclusion of this technical information does not necessarily imply endorsement by either the authors or the publisher.

8251A
PROGRAMMABLE COMMUNICATION INTERFACE

- **Synchronous and Asynchronous Operation**
  - **Synchronous:**
    5-8 Bit Characters
    Internal or External Character Synchronization
    Automatic Sync Insertion
  - **Asynchronous:**
    5-8 Bit Characters
    Clock Rate — 1, 16 or 64 Times Baud Rate
    Break Character Generation
    1, 1½, or 2 Stop Bits
    False Start Bit Detection
    Automatic Break Detect and Handling

- **Baud Rate —DC to 64k Baud**
- **Full Duplex, Double Buffered, Transmitter and Receiver**
- **Error Detection — Parity, Overrun, and Framing**
- **Fully Compatible with 8080/8085 CPU**
- **28-Pin DIP Package**
- **All Inputs and Outputs Are TTL Compatible**
- **Single 5 Volt Supply**
- **Single TTL Clock**

The 8251A is the enhanced version of the industry standard, Intel® 8251 Universal Synchronous/Asynchronous Receiver/Transmitter (USART), designed for data communications with Intel's new high performance family of microprocessors such as the 8085. The 8251A is used as a peripheral device and is programmed by the CPU to operate using virtually any serial data transmission technique presently in use (including IBM Bi-Sync). The USART accepts data characters from the CPU in parallel format and then converts them into a continuous serial data stream for transmission. Simultaneously, it can receive serial data streams and convert them into parallel data characters for the CPU. The USART will signal the CPU whenever it can accept a new character for transmission or whenever it has received a character for the CPU. The CPU can read the complete status of the USART at any time. These include data transmission errors and control signals such as SYNDET, TxEMPTY. The chip is constructed using N-channel silicon gate technology.

PIN CONFIGURATION

BLOCK DIAGRAM

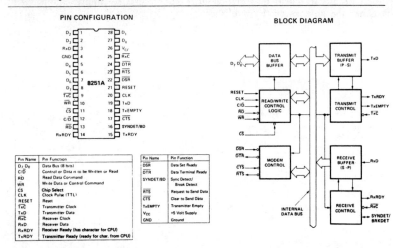

Pin Name	Pin Function
D$_7$ D$_0$	Data Bus (8 bits)
C/$\overline{\text{D}}$	Control or Data is to be Written or Read
$\overline{\text{RD}}$	Read Data Command
$\overline{\text{WR}}$	Write Data or Control Command
$\overline{\text{CS}}$	Chip Select
CLK	Clock Pulse (TTL)
RESET	Reset
$\overline{\text{TxC}}$	Transmitter Clock
TxD	Transmitter Data
$\overline{\text{RxC}}$	Receiver Clock
RxD	Receiver Data
RxRDY	Receiver Ready (has character for CPU)
TxRDY	Transmitter Ready (ready for char. from CPU)

Pin Name	Pin Function
$\overline{\text{DSR}}$	Data Set Ready
$\overline{\text{DTR}}$	Data Terminal Ready
SYNDET/BD	Sync Detect/ Break Detect
$\overline{\text{RTS}}$	Request to Send Data
$\overline{\text{CTS}}$	Clear to Send Data
TxEMPTY	Transmitter Empty
V$_{CC}$	+5 Volt Supply
GND	Ground

8251A BASIC FUNCTIONAL DESCRIPTION

General

The 8251A is a Universal Synchronous/Asynchronous Receiver/Transmitter designed specifically for the 80/85 Microcomputer Systems. Like other I/O devices in a Microcomputer System, its functional configuration is programmed by the system's software for maximum flexibility. The 8251A can support virtually any serial data technique currently in use (including IBM "bi-sync").

In a communication environment an interface device must convert parallel format system data into serial format for transmission and convert incoming serial format data into parallel system data for reception. The interface device must also delete or insert bits or characters that are functionally unique to the communication technique. In essence, the interface should appear "transparent" to the CPU, a simple input or output of byte-oriented system data.

Data Bus Buffer

This 3-state, bidirectional, 8-bit buffer is used to interface the 8251A to the system Data Bus. Data is transmitted or received by the buffer upon execution of INput or OUTput instructions of the CPU. Control words, Command words and Status information are also transferred through the Data Bus Buffer. The command status and data in, and data out are separate 8-bit registers to provide double buffering.

This functional block accepts inputs from the system Control bus and generates control signals for overall device operation. It contains the Control Word Register and Command Word Register that store the various control formats for the device functional definition.

RESET (Reset)

A "high" on this input forces the 8251A into an "Idle" mode. The device will remain at "Idle" until a new set of control words is written into the 8251A to program its functional definition. Minimum RESET pulse width is 6 t_{CY} (clock must be running).

CLK (Clock)

The CLK input is used to generate internal device timing and is normally connected to the Phase 2 (TTL) output of the 8224 Clock Generator. No external inputs or outputs are referenced to CLK but the frequency of CLK must be greater than 30 times the Receiver or Transmitter data bit rates.

$\overline{WR}$ (Write)

A "low" on this input informs the 8251A that the CPU is writing data or control words to the 8251A.

$\overline{RD}$ (Read)

A "low" on this input informs the 8251A that the CPU is reading data or status information from the 8251A.

C/$\overline{D}$ (Control/Data)

This input, in conjunction with the $\overline{WR}$ and $\overline{RD}$ inputs, informs the 8251A that the word on the Data Bus is either a data character, control word or status information.
1 = CONTROL/STATUS   0 = DATA

$\overline{CS}$ (Chip Select)

A "low" on this input selects the 8251A. No reading or writing will occur unless the device is selected. When $\overline{CS}$ is high, the Data Bus in the float state and $\overline{RD}$ and $\overline{WR}$ will have no effect on the chip.

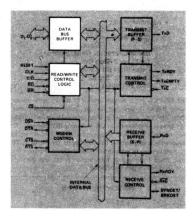

C/$\overline{D}$	$\overline{RD}$	$\overline{WR}$	$\overline{CS}$	
0	0	1	0	8251A DATA → DATA BUS
0	1	0	0	DATA BUS → 8251A DATA
1	0	1	0	STATUS → DATA BUS
1	1	0	0	DATA BUS → CONTROL
X	1	1	0	DATA BUS → 3-STATE
X	X	X	1	DATA BUS → 3-STATE

Modem Control

The 8251A has a set of control inputs and outputs that can be used to simplify the interface to almost any Modem. The Modem control signals are general purpose in nature and can be used for functions other than Modem control, if necessary.

$\overline{DSR}$ (Data Set Ready)

The $\overline{DSR}$ input signal is a general purpose, 1-bit inverting input port. Its condition can be tested by the CPU using a Status Read operation. The $\overline{DSR}$ input is normally used to test Modem conditions such as Data Set Ready.

$\overline{DTR}$ (Data Terminal Ready)

The $\overline{DTR}$ output signal is a general purpose, 1-bit inverting output port. It can be set "low" by programming the appropriate bit in the Command Instruction word. The $\overline{DTR}$ output signal is normally used for Modem control such as Data Terminal Ready or Rate Select.

$\overline{RTS}$ (Request to Send)

The $\overline{RTS}$ output signal is a general purpose, 1-bit inverting output port. It can be set "low" by programming the appropriate bit in the Command Instruction word. The $\overline{RTS}$ output signal is normally used for Modem control such as Request to Send.

$\overline{CTS}$ (Clear to Send)

A "low" on this input enables the 8251A to transmit serial data if the Tx Enable bit in the Command byte is set to a "one." If either a Tx Enable off or CTS off condition occurs while the Tx is in operation, the Tx will transmit all the data in the USART, written prior to Tx Disable command before shutting down.

Transmitter Buffer

The Transmitter Buffer accepts parallel data from the Data Bus Buffer, converts it to a serial bit stream, inserts the appropriate characters or bits (based on the communication technique) and outputs a composite serial stream of data on the TxD output pin on the falling edge of $\overline{TxC}$. The transmitter will begin transmission upon being enabled if $\overline{CTS}$ = 0. The TxD line will be held in the marking state immediately upon a master Reset or when Tx Enable/ $\overline{CTS}$ off or TxEMPTY.

Transmitter Control

The transmitter Control manages all activities associated with the transmission of serial data. It accepts and issues signals both externally and internally to accomplish this function.

TxRDY (Transmitter Ready)

This output signals the CPU that the transmitter is ready to accept a data character. The TxRDY output pin can be used as an interrupt to the system, since it is masked by Tx Disabled, or, for Polled operation, the CPU can check TxRDY using a Status Read operation. TxRDY is automatically reset by the leading edge of $\overline{WR}$ when a data character is loaded from the CPU.

Note that when using the Polled operation, the TxRDY status bit is *not* masked by Tx Enabled, but will only indicate the Empty/Full Status of the Tx Data Input Register.

TxE (Transmitter Empty)

When the 8251A has no characters to transmit, the TxEMP-TY output will go "high". It resets automatically upon receiving a character from the CPU. TxEMPTY can be used to indicate the end of a transmission mode, so that the CPU "knows" when to "turn the line around" in the half-duplexed operational mode. TxEMPTY is independent of the Tx Enable bit in the Command instruction.

In SYNChronous mode, a "high" on this output indicates that a character has not been loaded and the SYNC character or characters are about to be or are being transmitted automatically as "fillers". TxEMPTY does not go low when the SYNC characters are being shifted out.

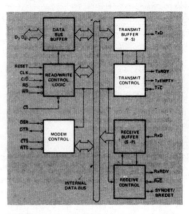

$\overline{TxC}$ (Transmitter Clock)

The Transmitter Clock controls the rate at which the character is to be transmitted. In the Synchronous transmission mode, the Baud Rate (1x) is equal to the $\overline{TxC}$ frequency. In Asynchronous transmission mode the baud rate is a fraction of the actual $\overline{TxC}$ frequency. A portion of the mode instruction selects this factor; it can be 1, 1/16 or 1/64 the $\overline{TxC}$.

For Example:

> If Baud Rate equals 110 Baud,
> $\overline{TxC}$ equals 110 Hz (1x)
> $\overline{TxC}$ equals 1.76 kHz (16x)
> $\overline{TxC}$ equals 7.04 kHz (64x).

The falling edge of $\overline{TxC}$ shifts the serial data out of the 8251A.

Receiver Buffer

The Receiver accepts serial data, converts this serial input to parallel format, checks for bits or characters that are unique to the communication technique and sends an "assembled" character to the CPU. Serial data is input to RxD pin, and is clocked in on the rising edge of $\overline{RxC}$.

Receiver Control

This functional block manages all receiver-related activities which consist of the following features:

The RxD initialization circuit prevents the 8251A from mistaking an unused input line for an active low data line in the "break condition". Before starting to receive serial characters on the RxD line, a valid "1" must first be detected after a chip master Reset. Once this has been determined, a search for a valid low (Start bit) is enabled. This feature is only active in the asynchronous mode, and is only done once for each master Reset.

The False Start bit detection circuit prevents false starts due to a transient noise spike by first detecting the falling edge and then strobing the nominal center of the Start bit (RxD = low).

The Parity Toggle F/F and Parity Error F/F circuits are used for parity error detection and set the corresponding status bit.

The Framing Error Flag F/F is set if the Stop bit is absent at the end of the data byte (asynchronous mode), and also sets the corresponding status bit.

RxRDY (Receiver Ready)

This output indicates that the 8251A contains a character that is ready to be input to the CPU. Rx RDY can be connected to the interrupt structure of the CPU or, for Polled operation, the CPU can check the condition of RxRDY using a Status Read operation.

Rx Enable off both masks and holds RxRDY in the Reset Condition. For Asynchronous mode, to set RxRDY, the Receiver must be Enabled to sense a Start Bit and a complete character must be assembled and transferred to the Data Output Register. For Synchronous mode, to set RxRDY, the Receiver must be enabled and a character must finish assembly and be transferred to the Data Output Register.

Failure to read the received character from the Rx Data Output Register prior to the assembly of the next Rx Data character will set overrun condition error and the previous character will be written over and lost. If the Rx Data is being read by the CPU when the internal transfer is occurring, overrun error will be set and the old character will be lost.

$\overline{RxC}$ (Receiver Clock)

The Receiver Clock controls the rate at which the character is to be received. In Synchronous Mode, the Baud Rate (1x) is equal to the actual frequency of $\overline{RxC}$. In Asynchronous Mode, the Baud Rate is a fraction of the actual $\overline{RxC}$ fre-

quency. A portion of the mode instruction selects this factor; 1, 1/16 or 1/64 the $\overline{RxC}$.

For Example:

Baud Rate equals 300 Baud, if
$\overline{RxC}$ equals 300 Hz (1x)
$\overline{RxC}$ equals 4800 Hz (16x)
$\overline{RxC}$ equals 19.2 kHz (64x).

Baud Rate equals 2400 Baud, if
$\overline{RxC}$ equals 2400 Hz (1x)
$\overline{RxC}$ equals 38.4 kHz (16x)
$\overline{RxC}$ equals 153.6 kHz (64x).

Data is sampled into the 8251A on the rising edge of $\overline{RxC}$.

NOTE: In most communications systems, the 8251A will be handling both the transmission and reception operations of a single link. Consequently, the Receive and Transmit Baud Rates will be the same. Both $\overline{TxC}$ and $\overline{RxC}$ will require identical frequencies for this operation and can be tied together and connected to a single frequency source (Baud Rate Generator) to simplify the interface.

SYNDET (SYNC Detect)/BRKDET (Break Detect)

This pin is used in SYNChronous Mode for SYNDET and may be used as either input or output, programmable through the Control Word. It is reset to output mode low upon RESET. When used as an output (internal Sync mode), the SYNDET pin will go "high" to indicate that the 8251A has located the SYNC character in the Receive mode. If the 8251A is programmed to use double Sync characters (bi-sync), then SYNDET will go "high" in the middle of the last bit of the second Sync character. SYNDET is automatically reset upon a Status Read operation.

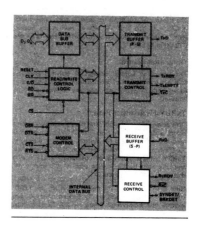

When used as an input (external SYNC detect mode), a positive going signal will cause the 8251A to start assembling data characters on the rising edge of the next $\overline{RxC}$. Once in SYNC, the "high" input signal can be removed. the period of $\overline{RxC}$. When External SYNC Detect is programmed, the Internal SYNC Detect is disabled.

Break Detect (Async Mode Only)

This output will go high whenever an all zero word of the programmed length (including start bit, data bit, parity bit, and *one* stop bit) is received. Break Detect may also be read as a Status bit. It is reset only upon a master chip Reset or Rx Data returning to a "one" state.

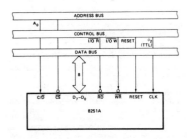

8251A Interface to 8080 Standard System Bus

DETAILED OPERATION DESCRIPTION

General

The complete functional definition of the 8251A is programmed by the system's software. A set of control words must be sent out by the CPU to initialize the 8251A to support the desired communications format. These control words will program the: BAUD RATE, CHARACTER LENGTH, NUMBER OF STOP BITS, SYNCHRONOUS or ASYNCHRONOUS OPERATION, EVEN/ODD/OFF PARITY, etc. In the Synchronous Mode, options are also provided to select either internal or external character synchronization.

Once programmed, the 8251A is ready to perform its communication functions. The TxRDY output is raised "high" to signal the CPU that the 8251A is ready to receive a data character from the CPU. This output (TxRDY) is reset automatically when the CPU writes a character into the 8251A. On the other hand, the 8251A receives serial data from the MODEM or I/O device. Upon receiving an entire character, the RxRDY output is raised "high" to signal the CPU that the 8251A has a complete character ready for the CPU to fetch. RxRDY is reset automatically upon the CPU data read operation.

The 8251A cannot begin transmission until the Tx Enable (Transmitter Enable) bit is set in the Command Instruction and it has received a Clear To Send ($\overline{CTS}$) input. The TxD output will be held in the marking state upon Reset.

Programming the 8251A

Prior to starting data transmission or reception, the 8251A must be loaded with a set of control words generated by the CPU. These control signals define the complete functional definition of the 8251A and must immediately follow a Reset operation (internal or external).

The control words are split into two formats:

1. Mode Instruction
2. Command Instruction

Mode Instruction

This format defines the general operational characteristics of the 8251A. It must follow a Reset operation (internal or external). Once the Mode Instruction has been written into the 8251A by the CPU, SYNC characters or Command Instructions may be inserted.

Command Instruction

This format defines a status word that is used to control the actual operation of the 8251A.

Both the Mode and Command Instructions must conform to a specified sequence for proper device operation. The Mode Instruction must be inserted immediately following a Reset operation, prior to using the 8251A for data communication.

All control words written into the 8251A after the Mode Instruction will load the Command Instruction. Command Instructions can be written into the 8251A at any time in the data block during the operation of the 8251A. To return to the Mode Instruction format, the master Reset bit in the Command Instruction word can be set to initiate an internal Reset operation which automatically places the 8251A back into the Mode Instruction format. Command Instructions must follow the Mode Instructions or Sync characters.

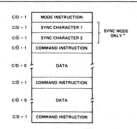

* The second SYNC character is skipped if MODE instruction has programmed the 8251A to single character Internal SYNC Mode. Both SYNC characters are skipped if MODE instruction has programmed the 8251A to ASYNC mode.

Typical Data Block

Mode Instruction Definition

The 8251A can be used for either Asynchronous or Synchronous data communication. To understand how the Mode Instruction defines the functional operation of the 8251A, the designer can best view the device as two separate components sharing the same package, one Asynchronous the other Synchronous. The format definition can be changed only after a master chip Reset. For explanation purposes the two formats will be isolated.

NOTE: When parity is enabled it is not considered as one of the data bits for the purpose of programming the word length. The actual parity bit received on the Rx Data line cannot be read on the Data Bus. In the case of a programmed character length of less than 8 bits, the least significant Data Bus bits will hold the data; unused bits are "don't care" when writing data to the 8251A, and will be "zeros" when reading the data from the 8251A.

Asynchronous Mode (Transmission)

Whenever a data character is sent by the CPU the 8251A automatically adds a Start bit (low level) followed by the data bits (least significant bit first), and the programmed number of Stop bits to each character. Also, an even or odd Parity bit is inserted prior to the Stop bit(s), as defined by the Mode Instruction. The character is then transmitted as a serial data stream on the TxD output. The serial data is shifted out on the falling edge of $\overline{TxC}$ at a rate equal to 1, 1/16, or 1/64 that of the $\overline{TxC}$, as defined by the Mode Instruction. BREAK characters can be continuously sent to the TxD if commanded to do so.

When no data characters have been loaded into the 8251A the TxD output remains "high" (marking) unless a Break (continuously low) has been programmed.

Asynchronous Mode (Receive)

The RxD line is normally high. A falling edge on this line triggers the beginning of a START bit. The validity of this START bit is checked by again strobing this bit at its nominal center (16X or 64X mode only). If a low is detected again, it is a valid START bit, and the bit counter will start counting. The bit counter thus locates the center of the data bits, the parity bit (if it exists) and the stop bits. If parity error occurs, the parity error flag is set. Data and parity bits are sampled on the RxD pin with the rising edge of $\overline{RxC}$. If a low level is detected as the STOP bit, the Framing Error flag will be set. The STOP bit signals the end of a character. Note that the *receiver* requires only *one* stop bit, regardless of the number of stop bits programmed. This character is then loaded into the parallel I/O buffer of the 8251A. The RxRDY pin is raised to signal the CPU that a character is ready to be fetched. If a previous character has not been fetched by the CPU, the present character replaces it in the I/O buffer, and the OVERRUN Error flag is raised (thus the previous character is lost). All of the error flags can be reset by an Error Reset Instruction. The occurrence of any of these errors will not affect the operation of the 8251A.

Mode Instruction Format, Asynchronous Mode

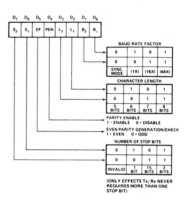

Asynchronous Mode

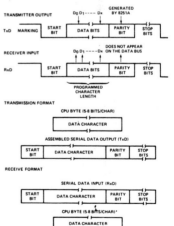

Synchronous Mode (Transmission)

The TxD output is continuously high until the CPU sends its first character to the 8251A which usually is a SYNC character. When the $\overline{\text{CTS}}$ line goes low, the first character is serially transmitted out. All characters are shifted out on the falling edge of $\overline{\text{TxC}}$. Data is shifted out at the same rate as the $\overline{\text{TxC}}$.

Once transmission has started, the data stream at the TxD output must continue at the $\overline{\text{TxC}}$ rate. If the CPU does not provide the 8251A with a data character before the 8251A Transmitter Buffers become empty, the SYNC characters (or character if in single SYNC character mode) will be automatically inserted in the TxD data stream. In this case, the TxEMPTY pin is raised high to signal that the 8251A is empty and SYNC characters are being sent out. TxEMPTY does not go low when the SYNC is being shifted out (see figure below). The TxEMPTY pin is internally reset by a data character being written into the 8251A.

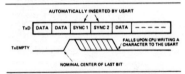

Synchronous Mode (Receive)

In this mode, character synchronization can be internally or externally achieved. If the SYNC mode has been programmed, ENTER HUNT command should be included in the first command instruction word written. Data on the RxD pin is then sampled in on the rising edge of $\overline{\text{RxC}}$. The content of the Rx buffer is compared at every bit boundary with the first SYNC character until a match occurs. If the 8251A has been programmed for two SYNC characters, the subsequent received character is also compared; when both SYNC characters have been detected, the USART ends the HUNT mode and is in character synchronization. The SYNDET pin is then set high, and is reset automatically by a STATUS READ. If parity is programmed, SYNDET will not be set until the middle of the parity bit instead of the middle of the last data bit.

In the external SYNC mode, synchronization is achieved by applying a high level on the SYNDET pin, thus forcing the 8251A out of the HUNT mode. The high level can be removed after one $\overline{\text{RxC}}$ cycle. An ENTER HUNT command has no effect in the asynchronous mode of operation.

Parity error and overrun error are both checked in the same way as in the Asynchronous Rx mode. Parity is checked when not in Hunt, regardless of whether the Receiver is enabled or not.

The CPU can command the receiver to enter the HUNT mode if synchronization is lost. This will also set all the used character bits in the buffer to a "one", thus preventing a possible false SYNDET caused by data that happens to be in the Rx Buffer at ENTER HUNT time. Note that

the SYNDET F/F is reset at each Status Read, regardless of whether internal or external SYNC has been programmed. This does not cause the 8251A to return to the HUNT mode. When in SYNC mode, but not in HUNT, Sync Detection is still functional, but only occurs at the "known" word boundaries. Thus, if one Status Read indicates SYNDET and a second Status Read also indicates SYNDET, then the programmed SYNDET characters have been received since the previous Status Read. (If double character sync has been programmed, then both sync characters have been contiguously received to gate a SYNDET indication.) When external SYNDET mode is selected, internal Sync Detect is disabled, and the SYNDET F/F may be set at any bit boundary.

Mode Instruction Format

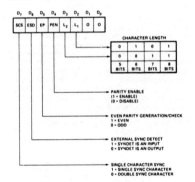

Data Format, Synchronous Mode

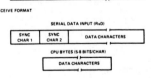

COMMAND INSTRUCTION DEFINITION

Once the functional definition of the 8251A has been programmed by the Mode Instruction and the Sync Characters are loaded (if in Sync Mode) then the device is ready to be used for data communication. The Command Instruction controls the actual operation of the selected format. Functions such as: Enable Transmit/Receive, Error Reset and Modem Controls are provided by the Command Instruction.

Once the Mode Instruction has been written into the 8251A and Sync characters inserted, if necessary, then all further "control writes" (C/$\overline{D}$ = 1) will load a Command Instruction. A Reset Operation (internal or external) will return the 8251A to the Mode Instruction format.

STATUS READ DEFINITION

In data communication systems it is often necessary to examine the "status" of the active device to ascertain if errors have occurred or other conditions that require the processor's attention. The 8251A has facilities that allow the programmer to "read" the status of the device at any time during the functional operation. (The status update is inhibited during status read).

A normal "read" command is issued by the CPU with C/$\overline{D}$ = 1 to accomplish this function.

Some of the bits in the Status Read Format have identical meanings to external output pins so that the 8251A can be used in a completely Polled environment or in an interrupt driven environment. TxRDY is an exception.

Note that status update can have a maximum delay of 28 clock periods from the actual event affecting the status.

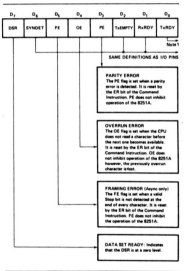

D$_7$	D$_6$	D$_5$	D$_4$	D$_3$	D$_2$	D$_1$	D$_0$
EH	IR	RTS	ER	SBRK	RxE	DTR	TxEN

TRANSMIT ENABLE
1 = enable
0 = disable

DATA TERMINAL READY
"high" will force $\overline{DTR}$ output to zero

RECEIVE ENABLE
1 = enable
0 = disable

SEND BREAK CHARACTER
1 = forces TxD "low"
0 = normal operation

ERROR RESET
1 = reset error flags PE, OE, FE

REQUEST TO SEND
"high" will force $\overline{RTS}$ output to zero

INTERNAL RESET
"high" returns 8251A to Mode Instruction Format

ENTER HUNT MODE*
1 = enable search for Sync Characters

* (HAS NO EFFECT IN ASYNC MODE)

Note: Error Reset must be performed whenever RxEnable and Enter Hunt are programmed.

Command Instruction Format

D$_7$	D$_6$	D$_5$	D$_4$	D$_3$	D$_2$	D$_1$	D$_0$
DSR	SYNDET	FE	OE	PE	TxEMPTY	RxRDY	TxRDY

Note 1

SAME DEFINITIONS AS I/O PINS

PARITY ERROR
The PE flag is set when a parity error is detected. It is reset by the ER bit of the Command Instruction. PE does not inhibit operation of the 8251A.

OVERRUN ERROR
The OE flag is set when the CPU does not read a character before the next one becomes available. It is reset by the ER bit of the Command Instruction. OE does not inhibit operation of the 8251A however, the previously overrun character is lost.

FRAMING ERROR (Async only)
The FE flag is set when a valid Stop bit is not detected at the end of every character. It is reset by the ER bit of the Command Instruction. FE does not inhibit the operation of the 8251A.

DATA SET READY: Indicates that the DSR is at a zero level.

Status Read Format

Note 1: TxRDY status bit has different meanings from the TxRDY output pin. The former is not conditioned by $\overline{CTS}$ and TxEN; the latter is conditioned by both $\overline{CTS}$ and TxEN.

i.e. TxRDY status bit = DB Buffer Empty

TxRDY pin out = DB Buffer Empty · (CTS=0) · (TxEN=1)

Data Sheet for
PCI 2651 USART IC

A data sheet (abridged) for the Signetics Programmable Communications Interface (PCI) 2651 USART integrated circuit. *Courtesy of Signetics Corporation, Sunnyvale, CA.*

These data sheets have been provided for general informational use only. Complete up-to-date data sheets should be obtained directly from the manufacturer for additional information and complete electrical specifications. Inclusion of this technical information does not necessarily imply endorsement by either the authors or the publisher.

DESCRIPTION

The Signetics 2651 PCI is a universal synchronous/asychronous data communications controller chip designed for microcomputer systems. It interfaces directly to the Signetics 2650 microprocessor and may be used in a polled or interrupt driven system environment. The 2651 accepts programmed instructions from the microprocessor and supports many serial data communication disciplines, synchronous and asynchronous, in the full or half-duplex mode.

The PCI serializes parallel data characters received from the microprocessor for transmission. Simultaneously, it can receive serial data and convert it into parallel data characters for input to the microcomputer.

The 2651 contains a baud rate generator which can be programmed to either accept an external clock or to generate internal transmit or receive clocks. Sixteen different baud rates can be selected under program control when operating in the internal clock mode.

The PCI is constructed using Signetics n-channel silicon gate depletion load technology and is packaged in a 28-pin DIP.

FEATURES

- **Synchronous operation**
  - 5 to 8-bit characters
  - Single or double SYN operation
  - Internal character synchronization
  - Transparent or non-transparent mode
  - Automatic SYN or DLE-SYN insertion
  - SYN or DLE stripping
  - Odd, even, or no parity
  - Local or remote maintenance loop back mode
  - Baud rate: dc to 0.8M baud (1X clock)

- **Asynchronous operation**
  - 5 to 8-bit characters
  - 1, 1 1/2 or 2 stop bits
  - Odd, even, or no parity
  - Parity, overrun and framing error detection
  - Line break detection and generation
  - False start bit detection
  - Automatic serial echo mode
  - Local or remote maintenance loop back mode
  - Baud rate: dc to 0.8M baud (1X clock)
  - dc to 50K baud (16X clock)
  - dc to 12.5K baud (64X clock)

OTHER FEATURES

- Internal or external baud rate clock
- 16 internal rates-50 to 19,200 baud
- Double buffered transmitter and receiver
- Full or half duplex operation
- Fully compatible with 2650 CPU
- TTL compatible inputs and outputs
- Single 5V power supply
- No system clock required
- 28-pin dual in-line package

APPLICATIONS

- Intelligent terminals
- Network processors
- Front end processors
- Remote data concentrators
- Computer to computer links
- Serial peripherals

PIN CONFIGURATION

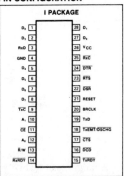

I PACKAGE

PIN DESIGNATION

PIN NO.	SYMBOL	NAME & FUNCTION	TYPE
27,28,1,2, 5-8	D_0-D_7	8-bit data bus	I/O
21	RESET	Reset	I
12,10	A_0-A_1	Internal register select lines	I
13	R̄/W	Read or write command	I
11	C̄Ē	Chip enable input	I
22	D̄S̄R̄	Data set ready	I
24	D̄T̄R̄	Data terminal ready	O
23	R̄T̄S̄	Request to send	O
17	C̄T̄S̄	Clear to send	I
16	D̄C̄D̄	Data carrier detected	I
18	TxEMT/DSCHG	Transmitter empty or data set change	O
9	T̄x̄C̄	Transmitter clock	I/O
25	R̄x̄C̄	Receiver clock	I/O
19	TxD	Transmitter data	O
3	RxD	Receiver data	I
15	T̄x̄R̄D̄Ȳ	Transmitter ready	O
14	R̄x̄R̄D̄Ȳ	Receiver ready	O
20	BRCLK	Baud rate generator clock	I
26	V_{CC}	+5V supply	I
4	GND	Ground	I

BLOCK DIAGRAM

The PCI consists of six major sections. These are the transmitter, receiver, timing, operation control, modem control and SYN/DLE control. These sections communicate with each other via an internal data bus and an internal control bus. The internal data bus interfaces to the microprocessor data bus via a data bus buffer.

Operation Control

This functional block stores configuration and operation commands from the CPU and generates appropriate signals to various internal sections to control the overall device operation. It contains read and write circuits to permit communications with the microprocessor via the data bus and contains Mode Registers 1 and 2, the Command Reg-

PRELIMINARY SPECIFICATION   2651-I

Baud Rate	Theoretical Frequency 16X Clock	Actual Frequency 16X Clock	Percent Error	Duty Cycle %	Divisor
50	0.8 KHz	0.8 KHz	--	50/50	6336
75	1.2	1.2	--	50/50	4224
110	1.76	1.76	--	50/50	2880
134.5	2.152	2.1523	0.016	50/50	2355
150	2.4	2.4	--	50/50	2112
300	4.8	4.8	--	50/50	1056
600	9.6	9.6	--	50/50	528
1200	19.2	19.2	--	50/50	264
1800	28.8	28.8	--	50/50	176
2000	32.0	32.081	0.253	50/50	158
2400	38.4	38.4	--	50/50	132
3600	57.6	57.6	--	50/50	88
4800	76.8	76.8	--	50/50	66
7200	115.2	115.2	--	50/50	44
9600	153.6	153.6	--	48/52	33
19200	307.2	316.8	3.125	50/50	16

NOTE

16X clock is used in asynchronous mode. In synchronous mode, clock multiplier is 1X and duty cycle is
50%/50% for any baud rate.

Table 1 BAUD RATE GENERATOR CHARACTERISTICS
Crystal Frequency = 5.0688MHz

PIN NAME	PIN NO.	INPUT/OUTPUT	FUNCTION
V_{CC}	26	I	+5V supply input
GND	4	I	Ground
RESET	21	I	A high on this input performs a master reset on the 2651. This signal asynchronously terminates any device activity and clears the Mode, Command and Status registers. The device assumes the idle state and remains there until initialized with the appropriate control words.
A_1-A_0	10,12	I	Address lines used to select internal PCI registers.
$\overline{R}$/W	13	I	Read command when low, write command when high.
$\overline{CE}$	11	I	Chip enable command. When low, indicates that control and data lines to the PCI are valid and that the operation specified by the $\overline{R}$/W, A_1 and A_0 inputs should be performed. When high, places the D_0-D_7 lines in the tri-state condition.
D_7-D_0	8,7,6,5, 2,1,28,27	I/O	8-bit, three-state data bus used to transfer commands, data and status between PCI and the CPU. D_0 is the least significant bit; D_7 the most significant bit.
$\overline{TxRDY}$	15	O	This output is the complement of Status Register bit SR0. When low, it indicates that the Transmit Data Holding Register (THR) is ready to accept a data character from the CPU. It goes high when the data character is loaded. This output is valid only when the transmitter is enabled. It is an open drain output which can be used as an interrupt to the CPU.
$\overline{RxRDY}$	14	O	This output is the complement of Status Register bit SR1. When low, it indicates that the Receive Data Holding Register (RHR) has a character ready for input to the CPU. It goes high when the RHR is read by the CPU, and also when the receiver is disabled. It is an open drain output which can be used as an interrupt to the CPU.
$\overline{TxEMT/DSCHG}$	18	O	This output is the complement of Status Register bit SR2. When low, it indicates that the transmitter has completed serialization of the last character loaded by the CPU, or that a change of state of the $\overline{DSR}$ or $\overline{DCD}$ inputs has occurred. This output goes high when the Status Register is read by the CPU, if the TxEMT condition does not exist. Otherwise, the THR must be loaded by the CPU for this line to go high. It is an open drain output which can be used as an interrupt to the CPU.

Table 2 CPU-RELATED SIGNALS

BLOCK DIAGRAM

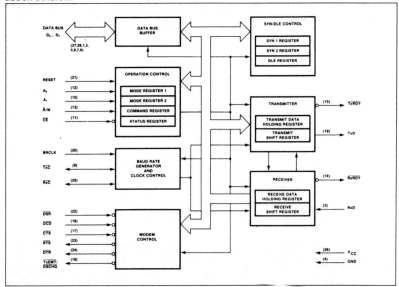

ister, and the Status Register. Details of register addressing and protocol are presented in the PCI PROGRAMMING section of this data sheet.

Timing
The PCI contains a Baud Rate Generator (BRG) which is programmable to accept external transmit or receive clocks or to divide an external clock to perform data communications: The unit can generate 16 commonly used baud rates, any one of which can be selected for full duplex operation. See Table 1.

Receiver
The Receiver accepts serial data on the RxD pin, converts this serial input to parallel format, checks for bits or characters that are unique to the communication technique and sends an "assembled" character to the CPU.

Transmitter
The Transmitter accepts parallel data from the CPU, converts it to a serial bit stream, inserts the appropriate characters or bits

(based on the communication technique) and outputs a composite serial stream of data on the TxD output pin.

Modem Control
The modem control section provides interfacing for three input signals and three output signals used for "handshaking" and status indication between the CPU and a modem.

SYN/DLE Control
This section contains control circuitry and three 8-bit registers storing the SYN1, SYN2, and DLE characters provided by the CPU. These registers are used in the synchronous mode of operation to provide the characters required for synchronization, idle fill and data transparency.

INTERFACE SIGNALS
The PCI interface signals can be grouped into two types: the CPU-related signals (shown in Table 2), which interface the 2651 to the microprocessor system, and the device-related signals (shown in Table 3), which are used to interface to the communi-

cations device or system.

OPERATION
The functional operation of the 2651 is programmed by a set of control words supplied by the CPU. These control words specify items such as synchronous or asynchronous mode, baud rate, number of bits per cha:acter, etc. The programming procedure is described in the PCI PROGRAMMING section of this data sheet.

After programming, the PCI is ready to perform the desired communications functions. The receiver performs serial to parallel conversion of data received from a modem or equivalent device. The transmitter converts parallel data received from the CPU to a serial bit stream. These actions are accomplished within the framework specified by the control words.

Receiver
The 2651 is conditioned to receive data when the $\overline{DCD}$ input is low and the RxEN bit in the command register is true. In the asynchronous mode, the receiver looks for

PIN NAME	PIN NO.	INPUT/OUTPUT	FUNCTION
BRCLK	20	I	5.0688MHz clock input to the internal baud rate generator. Not required if external receiver and transmitter clocks are used.
$\overline{RxC}$	25	I/O	Receiver clock. If external receiver clock is programmed, this input controls the rate at which the character is to be received. Its frequency is 1X, 16X or 64X the baud rate, as programmed by Mode Register 1. Data is sampled on the rising edge of the clock. If internal receiver clock is programmed, this pin becomes an output at 1X the programmed baud rate.
$\overline{TxC}$	9	I/O	Transmitter clock. If external transmitter clock is programmed, this input controls the rate at which the character is transmitted. Its frequency is 1X, 16X or 64X the baud rate, as programmed by Mode Register 1. The transmitted data changes on the falling edge of the clock. If internal transmitter clock is programmed, this pin becomes an output at 1X the programmed baud rate.
RxD	3	I	Serial data input to the receiver. "Mark" is high, "Space" is low.
TxD	19	O	Serial data output from the transmitter. "Mark" is high, "Space" is low. Held in Mark condition when the transmitter is disabled.
$\overline{DSR}$	22	I	General purpose input which can be used for Data Set Ready or Ring Indicator condition. Its complement appears as Status Register SR7. Causes a low output on $\overline{TxEMT/DSCHG}$ when its state changes.
$\overline{DCD}$	16	I	Data Carrier Detect input. Must be low in order for the receiver to operate. Its complement appears as Status Register bit SR6. Causes a low output on $\overline{TxEMT/DSCHG}$ when its state changes.
$\overline{CTS}$	17	I	Clear to Send input. Must be low in order for the transmitter to operate.
$\overline{DTR}$	24	O	General purpose output which is the complement of Command Register bit CR1. Normally used to indicate Data Terminal Ready.
$\overline{RTS}$	23	O	General purpose output which is the complement of Command Register bit CR5. Normally used to indicate Request to Send.

Table 3 DEVICE-RELATED SIGNALS

a high to low transition of the start bit on the RxD input line. If a transition is detected, the state of the RxD line is sampled again after a delay of one-half of a bit time. If RxD is now high, the search for a valid start bit is begun again. If RxD is still low, a valid start bit is assumed and the receiver continues to sample the input line at one bit time intervals until the proper number of data bits, the parity bit, and the stop bit(s) have been assembled. The data is then transferred to the Receive Data Holding Register, the RxRDY bit in the status register is set, and the $\overline{RxRDY}$ output is asserted. If the character length is less than 8 bits, the high order unused bits in the Holding Register are set to zero. The Parity Error, Framing Error, and Overrun Error status bits are set if required. If a break condition is detected (RxD is low for the entire character as well as the stop bit (s)), only one character consisting of all zeros (with the FE status bit set) will be transferred to the Holding Register. The RxD input must return to a high condition before a search for the next start bit begins.

When the PCI is initialized into the synchronous mode, the receiver first enters the hunt mode. In this mode, as data is shifted into the Receiver Shift Register a bit at a time, the contents of the register are compared to the contents of the SYN1 register. If the two are not equal, the next bit is shifted in and the comparison is repeated. When the two re-

gisters match, the hunt mode is terminated and character assembly mode begins. If single SYN operation is programmed, the SYN DETECT status bit is set. If double SYN operation is programmed, the first character assembled after SYN1 must be SYN2 in order for the SYN DETECT bit to be set. Otherwise, the PCI returns to the hunt mode. (Note that the sequence SYN1-SYN1-SYN2 will not achieve synchronization). When synchronization has been achieved, the PCI continues to assemble characters and transfer them to the Holding Register, setting the RxRDY output each time a character is transferred. The PE and OE status bits are set as appropriate. Further receipt of the appropriate SYN sequence sets the SYN DETECT status bit. If the SYN stripping mode is commanded, SYN characters are not transferred to the Holding Register. Note that the SYN characters used to establish initial synchronization are not transferred to the Holding Register in any case.

Transmitter

The PCI is conditioned to transmit data when the $\overline{CTS}$ input is low and the TxEN command register bit is set. The 2651 indicates to the CPU that it can accept a character for transmission by setting the TxRDY status bit and asserting the $\overline{TxRDY}$ output. When the CPU writes a character into the Transmit Data Holding Register, these

conditions are negated. Data is transferred from the Holding Register to the Transmit Shift Register when it is idle or has completed transmission of the previous character. The TxRDT conditions are then asserted again. Thus, one full character time of buffering is provided.

In the asynchronous mode, the transmitter automatically sends a start bit followed by the programmed number of data bits, the least significant bit being sent first. It then appends an optional odd or even parity bit and the programmed number of stop bits. If, following transmission of the stop bits, a new character is not available in the Transmit Holding Register, the TxD output remains in the marking (high) condition and the $\overline{TxEMT/DSCHG}$ output and its corresponding status bit are asserted. Transmission resumes when the CPU loads a new character into the Holding Register. The transmitter can be forced to output a continuous low (BREAK) condition by setting the Send Break command bit high.

In the synchronous mode, when the 2651 is initially conditioned to transmit, the TxD output remains high and the TxRDY condition is asserted until the first character to be transmitted (usually a SYN character) is loaded by the CPU. Subsequent to this, a continuous stream of characters is transmitted. No extra bits (other than parity, if commanded) are generated by the PCI

147

unless the CPU fails to send a new character to the PCI by the time the transmitter has completed sending the previous character. Since synchronous communications does not allow gaps between characters, the PCI asserts TxEMT and automatically "fills" the gap by transmitting SYN1s, SYN1-SYN2 doublets, or DLE-SYN1 doublets, depending on the command mode. Normal transmission of the message resumes when a new character is available in the Transmit Data Holding Register. If the SEND DLE bit in the command register is true, the DLE character is automatically transmitted prior to transmission of the message character.

PCI PROGRAMMING

Prior to initiating data communications, the 2651 operational mode must be programmed by performing write operations to the mode and command registers. In addition, if synchronous operation is programmed, the appropriate SYN/DLE registers must be loaded. The PCI can be reconfigured at any time during program execution. However, the receiver and transmitter should be disabled if the change has an effect on the reception or transmission of a character. A flowchart of the initialization process appears in Figure 1.

The internal registers of the PCI are accessed by applying specific signals to the CE, $\overline{R}/W$, A_1 and A_0 inputs. The conditions necessary to address each register are shown in Table 4.

The SYN1, SYN2, and DLE registers are accessed by performing write operations with the conditions $A_1 = 0$, $A_0 = 1$, and $\overline{R}/W = 1$. The first operation loads the SYN1 register. The next loads the SYN2 register, and the third loads the DLE register. Reading or loading the mode registers is done in a similar manner. The first write (or read) operation addresses Mode Register 1, and a subsequent operation addresses Mode Register 2. If more than the required number of accesses are made, the internal sequencer recycles to point at the first register. The pointers are reset to SYN1 Register and Mode Register 1 by a RESET input or by performing a "Read Command Register" operation, but are unaffected by any other read or write operation.

The 2651 register formats are summarized in Tables 5, 6, 7 and 8. Mode Registers 1 and 2 define the general operational characteristics of the PCI, while the Command Register controls the operation within this basic frame-work. The PCI indicates its status in the Status Register. These registers are cleared when a RESET input is applied.

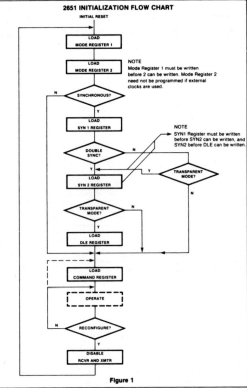

2651 INITIALIZATION FLOW CHART

INITIAL RESET

LOAD MODE REGISTER 1

LOAD MODE REGISTER 2

NOTE
Mode Register 1 must be written before 2 can be written. Mode Register 2 need not be programmed if external clocks are used.

SYNCHRONOUS?

LOAD SYN 1 REGISTER

NOTE
SYN1 Register must be written before SYN2 can be written, and SYN2 before DLE can be written.

DOUBLE SYNC?

TRANSPARENT MODE?

LOAD SYN 2 REGISTER

TRANSPARENT MODE?

LOAD DLE REGISTER

LOAD COMMAND REGISTER

OPERATE

RECONFIGURE?

DISABLE RCVR AND XMTR

Figure 1

$\overline{CE}$	A_1	A_0	$\overline{R}/W$	FUNCTION
1	X	X	X	Tri-state data bus
0	0	0	0	Read receive holding register
0	0	0	1	Write transmit holding register
0	0	1	0	Read status register
0	0	1	1	Write SYN1/SYN2/DLE registers
0	1	0	0	Read mode registers 1/2
0	1	0	1	Write mode registers 1/2
0	1	1	0	Read command register
0	1	1	1	Write command register

NOTE
See AC Characteristics section for timing requirements.

Table 4   2651 REGISTER ADDRESSING

MR17	MR16	MR15	MR14	MR13	MR12	MR11	MR10
		Parity Type	Parity Control	Character Length		Mode and Baud Rate Factor	
ASYNCH: STOP BIT LENGTH 00 = INVALID 01 = 1 STOP BIT 10 = 1½ STOP BITS 11 = 2 STOP BITS		0 = ODD 1 = EVEN	0 = DISABLED 1 = ENABLED	00 = 5 BITS 01 = 6 BITS 10 = 7 BITS 11 = 8 BITS		00 = SYNCHRONOUS 1X RATE 01 = ASYNCHRONOUS 1X RATE 10 = ASYNCHRONOUS 16X RATE 11 = ASYNCHRONOUS 64X RATE	
SYNCH: NUMBER OF SYN CHAR	SYNCH: TRANS-PARENCY CONTROL						
0 = DOUBLE SYN 1 = SINGLE SYN	0 = NORMAL 1 = TRANSPARENT						

NOTE
Baud rate factor in asynchronous applies only if external clock is selected. Factor is 16X if internal clock is selected.

Table 5 MODE REGISTER 1 (MR1)

MR27	MR26	MR25	MR24	MR23	MR22	MR21	MR20
		Transmitter Clock	Receiver Clock	Baud Rate Selection			
NOT USED		0 = EXTERNAL 1 = INTERNAL	0 = EXTERNAL 1 = INTERNAL	0000 = 50 BAUD 0001 = 75 0010 = 110 0011 = 134.5 0100 = 150 0101 = 300 0110 = 600 0111 = 1200		1000 = 1800 BAUD 1001 = 2000 1010 = 2400 1011 = 3600 1100 = 4800 1101 = 7200 1110 = 9600 1111 = 19,200	

Table 6 MODE REGISTER 2 (MR2)

Mode Register 1 (MR1)

Table 5 illustrates Mode Register 1. Bits MR11 and MR10 select the communication format and baud rate multiplier. 00 specifies synchronous mode and 1X multiplier. 1X, 16X, and 64X multipliers are programmable for asynchronous format. However, the multiplier in asynchronous format applies only if the external clock input option is selected by MR24 or MR25.

MR13 and MR12 select a character length of 5, 6, 7, or 8 bits. The character length does not include the parity bit, if programmed, and does not include the start and stop bits in asynchronous mode.

MR14 controls parity generation. If enabled, a parity bit is added to the transmitted character and the receiver performs a parity check on incoming data. MR15 selects odd or even parity when parity is enabled by MR14.

In asychronous mode, MR17 and MR16 select character framing of 1, 1.5, or 2 stop bits. (If 1X baud rate is programmed, 1.5 stop bits defaults to 2 stop bits on transmit.) In synchronous mode, MR17 controls the number of SYN characters used to establish synchronization and for character fill when the transmitter is idle. SYN1 alone is used if MR17 = 1, and SYN1-SYN2 is used when MR17 = 0. If the transparent mode is specified by MR16, DLE-SYN1 is used for character fill, but the normal synchronization sequence is used.

Mode Register 2 (MR2)

Table 6 illustrates Mode Register 2. MR23, MR22, MR21, and MR20 control the frequency of the internal baud rate generator (BRG). Sixteen rates are selectable. When driven by a 5.0688 MHz input at the BRCLK input (pin 20), the BRG output has zero error except at 134.5, 2000, and 19,200 baud, which have errors of +0.016%, +0.235%, and +3.125% respectively. The clock supplied to the receiver and transmitter (as selected by MR24 and MR25) has a 50%/50% duty cycle except in asynchronous mode, at 9600 baud, where the duty cycle is 48%/52%.

MR25 and MR24 select either the BRG or the external inputs TxC and RxC as the clock source for the transmitter and receiver, respectively. If the BRG clock is selected, the baud rate factor in asynchronous mode is 16X regardless of the factor selected by MR11 and MR10. In addition, the corresponding clock pin provides an output at 1X the baud rate.

Command Register (CR)

Table 7 illustrates Command Register. Bits CRO (TxEN) and CR2 (RxEN) enable or disable the transmitter and receiver respectively. If the transmitter is disabled, it will complete the transmission of the character in the Transmit Shift Register (if any) prior to terminating operation. The TxD output will then remain in the marking state (high). If the receiver is disabled, it will terminate operation immediately. Any character being assembled will be neglected.

Bits CR1 (DTR) and CR5 (RTS) control the DTR and RTS outputs. Data at the outputs is the logical complement of the register data.

In asynchronous mode, setting CR3 will force and hold the TxD output low (spacing condition) at the end of the current transmitted character. Normal operation resumes when CR3 is cleared. The TxD line will go high for a least one bit time before beginning transmission of the next character in the Transmit Data Holding Register. In synchronous mode, setting CR3 causes the transmission of the DLE register contents prior to sending the character in the Transmit Data Holding Register. CR3 should be reset in response to the next TxRDY.

Setting CR4 causes the error flags in the Status Register (SR3, SR4, and SR5) to be

149

CR7	CR6	CR5	CR4	CR3	CR2	CR1	CR0
Operating Mode		Request to Send	Reset Error		Receive Control (RxEN)	Data Terminal Ready	Transmit Control (TxEN)
00 = NORMAL OPERATION 01 = ASYNCH: AUTOMATIC ECHO MODE SYNCH: SYN AND/OR DLE STRIPPING MODE 10 = LOCAL LOOP BACK 11 = REMOTE LOOP BACK		0 = FORCE RTS OUTPUT HIGH 1 = FORCE RTS OUTPUT LOW	0 = NORMAL 1 = RESET ERROR FLAG IN STATUS REG (FE, OE, PE/DLE DETECT)	ASYNCH: FORCE BREAK 0 = NORMAL 1 = FORCE BREAK SYNCH: SEND DLE 0 = NORMAL 1 = SEND DLE	0 = DISABLE 1 = ENABLE	0 = FORCE DTR OUTPUT HIGH 1 = FORCE DTR OUTPUT LOW	0 = DISABLE 1 = ENABLE

Table 7 COMMAND REGISTER (CR)

SR7	SR6	SR5	SR4	SR3	SR2	SR1	SR0
Data Set Ready	Data Carrier Detect	FE/SYN Detect	Overrrun	PE/DLE Detect	TxEMT/DSCHG	RxRDY	TxRDY
0 = DSR INPUT IS HIGH 1 = DSR INPUT IS LOW	0 = DCD INPUT IS HIGH 1 = DCD INPUT IS LOW	ASYNCH: 0 = NORMAL 1 = FRAMING ERROR SYNCH: 0 = NORMAL 1 = SYN CHAR DETECTED	0 = NORMAL 1 = OVERRUN ERROR	ASYNCH: 0 = NORMAL 1 = PARITY ERROR SYNCH: 0 = NORMAL 1 = PARITY ERROR OR DLE CHAR RECEIVED	0 = NORMAL 1 = CHANGE IN DSR OR DCD, OR TRANSMIT SHIFT REGIS- TER IS EMPTY	0 = RECEIVE HOLDING REG EMPTY 1 = RECEIVE HOLDING REG HAS DATA	0 = TRANSMIT HOLDING REG BUSY 1 = TRANSMIT HOLDING REG EMPTY

Table 8 STATUS REGISTER (SR)

cleared. This bit resets automatically.

The PCI can operate in one of four sub-modes within each major mode (synchronous or asynchronous). The operational sub-mode is determined by CR7 and CR6. CR7–CR6 = 00 is the normal mode, with the transmitter and receiver operating independently in accordance with the Mode and Status Register instructions.

In asynchronous mode, CR7–CR6 = 01 places the PCI in the Automatic Echo mode. Clocked, regenerated received data is automatically directed to the TxD line while normal receiver operation continues. The receiver must be enabled (CR2 = 1), but the transmitter need not be enabled. CPU to receiver communications continues normally, but the CPU to transmitter link is disabled. Only the first character of a break condition is echoed. The TxD output will go high until the next valid start is detected. The following conditions are true while in Automatic Echo mode:

1. Data assembled by the receiver is automatically placed in the Transmit Holding Register and retransmitted by the transmitter on the TxD output.
2. Transmit clock = receive clock.
3. TxRDY output = 1.
4. The TxEMT/DSCHG pin will reflect only the data set change condition.

5. The TxEN command (CR0) is ignored.

In synchronous mode, CR7–CR6 = 01 places the PCI in the Automatic SYN/DLE Stripping mode. The exact action taken depends on the setting of bits MR17 and MR16:

1. In the non-transparent, single SYN mode (MR17–MR16 = 10), characters in the data stream matching SYN1 are not transferred to the Receive Data Holding Register (RHR).
2. In the non-transparent, double SYN mode (MR17–MR16 = 00), characters in the data stream matching SYN1, or SYN2 if immediately preceded by SYN1, are not transferred to the RHR. However, only the first SYN1 of an SYN1-SYN1 pair is stripped.
3. In transparent mode (MR16 =1), characters in the data stream matching DLE, or SYN1 if immediately preceded by DLE, are not transferred to the RHR. However, only the first DLE of a DLE-DLE pair is stripped.

Note that Automatic Stripping mode does not affect the setting of the DLE Detect and SYN Detect status bits (SR3 and SR5).

Two diagnostic sub-modes can also be configured. In Local Loop Back mode (CR7–CR6 = 10), the following loops are connected internally:

1. The transmitter output is connected to the receiver input.

2. DTR is connected to DCD and RTS is connect-ed to CTS.
3. Receive clock = transmit clock.
4. The DTR, RTS and TxD outputs are held high.
5. The CTS, DCD, DSR and RxD inputs are ig-nored.

Additional requirements to operate in the Local Loop Back mode are that CR0 (TxEN), CR1 (DTR), and CR5 (RTS) must be set to 1. CR2 (RxEN) is ignored by the PCI.

The second diagnostic mode is the Remote Loop Back mode (CR7–CR6 = 11). In this mode:

1. Data assembled by the receiver is automatically placed in the Transmit Holding Register and retransmitted by the transmitter on the TxD output.
2. Transmit clock = receive clock.
3. No data is sent to the local CPU, but the error status conditions (PE, OE, FE) are set.
4. The RxRDY, TxRDY, and TxEMT/DSCHG out-puts are held high.
5. CR1 (TxEN) is ignored.
6. All other signals operate normally.

Status Register

The data contained in the Status Register (as shown in Table 8) indicate receiver and transmitter conditions and modem/data set status.

PRELIMINARY SPECIFICATION 2651-I

SR0 is the Transmitter Ready (TxRDY) status bit. It, and its corresponding output, are valid only when the transmitter is enabled. If equal to 0, it indicates that the Transmit Data Holding Register has been loaded by the CPU and the data has not been transferred to the Transmit Shift Register. If set equal to 1, it indicates that the Holding Register is ready to accept data from the CPU. This bit is initially set when the Transmitter is enabled by CR0, unless a character has previously been loaded into the Holding Register. It is not set when the Automatic Echo or Remote Loop Back modes are programmed. When this bit is set, the TxRDY output pin is low. In the Automatic Echo and Remote Loop Back modes, the output is held high.

SR1, the Receiver Ready (RxRDY) status bit, indicates the condition of the Receive Data Holding Register. If set, it indicates that a character has been loaded into the Holding Register from the Receive Shift Register and is ready to be read by the CPU. If equal to zero, there is no new character in the Holding Register. This bit is cleared when the CPU reads the Receive Data Holding Register or when the receiver is disabled by CR2.

When set, the $\overline{RxRDY}$ output is low.

The TxEMT/DSCHG bit, SR2, when set, indicates either a change of state of the $\overline{DSR}$ or $\overline{DCD}$ inputs or that the Transmit Shift Register has completed transmission of a character and no new character has been loaded into the Transmit Data Holding Register. Note that in synchronous mode this bit will be set even though the appropriate "fill" character is transmitted. It is cleared when the transmitter is enabled by CR0 and does not indicate transmitter condition until at least one character is transmitted. It is also cleared when the Status Register is read by the CPU. When SR2 is set, the $\overline{TxEMT/-DSCHG}$ output is low.

SR3, when set, indicates a received parity error when parity is enabled by MR14. In synchronous transparent mode (MR16 = 1), with parity disabled, it indicates that a character matching the DLE Register has been received. However, only the first DLE of two successive DLEs will set SR3. This bit is cleared when the receiver is disabled and by the Reset Error command, CR4.

The Overrun Error status bit, SR4, indicates that the previous character loaded into the

Receive Holding Register was not read by the CPU at the time a new received character was transferred into it. This bit is cleared when the receiver is disabled and by the Reset Error command, CR4.

In asynchronous mode, bit SR5 signifies that the received character was not framed by the programmed number of stop bits. (If 1.5 stop bits are programmed, only the first stop bit is checked.) In synchronous non-transparent mode (MR16 = 0), it indicates receipt of the SYN1 character in single SYN mode or the SYN1-SYN2 pair in double SYN mode. In synchronous transparent mode (MR16 = 1), this bit is set upon detection of the initial synchronizing characters (SYN1 or SYN1-SYN2) and, after synchronization has been achieved, when a DLE-SYN1 pair is received. The bit is reset when the receiver is disabled, when the Reset Error command is given in asynchronous mode, and when the Status Register is read by the CPU in the synchronous mode.

$\overline{SR6}$ and $\overline{SR7}$ reflect the conditions of the $\overline{DCD}$ and $\overline{DSR}$ inputs respectively. A low input sets its corresponding status bit and a high input clears it.

ABSOLUTE MAXIMUM RATINGS[1]

PARAMETER	RATING	UNIT
Operating ambient temperature[2]	0 to +70	°C
Storage temperature	−65 to +150	°C
All voltages with respect to ground[3]	−0.5 to +6.0	V

PRELIMINARY SPECIFICATION

Manufacturer reserves the right to make design and process changes and improvements.

DC ELECTRICAL CHARACTERISTICS $T_A = 0°C$ to 70°C, $V_{CC} = 5.0V \pm 5\%$ [4,5,6,8]

	PARAMETER	TEST CONDITIONS	LIMITS			UNIT
			Min	Typ	Max	
V_{IL} V_{IH}	Input voltage Low High		2.0		0.8	V
V_{OL} V_{OH}	Output voltage Low High	$I_{OL} = 1.6mA$ $I_{OH} = -100uA$	2.4	0.25 2.8	0.45	V
I_{IL}	Input load current	$V_{IN} = 0$ to 5.5V			10	μA
I_{LD} I_{LO}	Output leakage current Data bus Open drain[7]	$V_{OUT} = 4.0V$ $V_{OUT} = 4.0V$			10 10	μA
I_{CC}	Power supply current			65	150	mA

PRELIMINARY SPECIFICATION

Manufacturer reserves the right to make design and process changes and improvements.

Overlay for LR-21 UART Outboard Module

An overlay diagram showing the positions of the various signals and their availability on the LR-21 UART Outboard module.

One 16-pin dual-in-line socket is dedicated to the data inputs and outputs. A flexible cable with 16-pin headers on each end may be used to simplify wiring to this socket. Another 16-pin dual-in-line socket provides access to the programming pins, the Control Strobe signal, the Received Data Enable, and the Status Word Enable control pins. A third socket provides access to other control pins, some of which are also brought to a series of pins that facilitate the use of the LR-21 Outboard module with solderless breadboard sockets (see also Figs. 36 and 37).

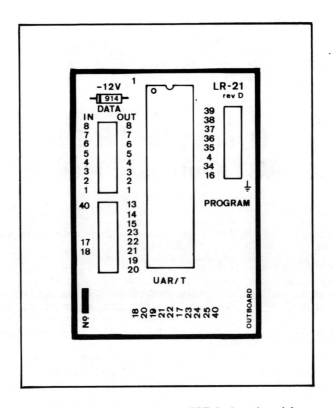

Fig. 50. Pin layout for LR-21 UART Outboard module.

Index

TO THE READER

This book is one of an expanding series of books that will cover the field of basic electronics and digital electronics from basic gates and flip-flops through microcomputers and digital telecommunications. We are attempting to develop a mailing list of individuals who would like to receive information on the series. We would be delighted to add your name to it if you would fill in the information below and mail this sheet to us. Thanks.

1. I have the following books:

_____

_____

_____

_____

_____

_____

_____

_____

_____

_____

_____

_____

2. My occupation is: ☐ student   ☐ teacher, instructor   ☐ hobbyist

   ☐ housewife   ☐ scientist, engineer, doctor, etc.   ☐ businessman

   ☐ Other: _____

Name (print): _____

Address _____

City _____ State _____

Zip Code _____

Mail to:

   Books
   P.O. Box 715
   Blacksburg, Virginia 24060